LOVE & MONEY

LOVE & MONEY

PROTECTING YOURSELF FROM ANGRY EXES, WACKY RELATIVES, CON ARTISTS, AND INNER DEMONS

ANN-MARGARET CARROZZA, ESQ.

ALLWORTH
PRESS

Allworth Press books may be purchased in bulk at special discounts for sales promotion, corporate gifts, fund-raising, or educational purposes. Special editions can also be created to specifications. For details, contact the Special Sales Department, Allworth Press, 307 West 36th Street, 11th Floor, New York, NY 10018 or info@skyhorsepublishing.com.

20 19 18 17 16 . . . 5 4 3 2 1

Published by Allworth Press, an imprint of Skyhorse Publishing, Inc.
307 West 36th Street, 11th Floor, New York, NY 10018.

Allworth Press® is a registered trademark of Skyhorse Publishing, Inc.®, a Delaware corporation.

www.allworth.com

Cover design by Brian Peterson
Cover photo credit Douglas Gorenstein

Library of Congress Cataloging-in-Publication Data is available on file.

Print ISBN: 978-1-62153-554-6
Ebook ISBN: 978-1-62153-563-8

Printed in the United States of America

For Bill, Billy, and Danny

TABLE OF CONTENTS

FOREWORD BY DR. PHIL

In *Love and Money*, Ann-Margaret Carrozza, a preeminent asset protection attorney, teaches us how to keep those people with "larceny in their hearts" out of our pockets, bank accounts, retirement funds, and every other accumulation of our hard-earned money. Sometimes those who seek to redistribute the fruits of your labors are those closest to you, those with whom you have been the most intertwined. Across forty-plus years in dealing with relationships, I have observed that people certainly divorce a different person than they marry! Ann-Margaret teaches us that the old saying is true: "Good fences make good neighbors." More important, in *Love and Money* she teaches us all when, where, and how to build those fences.

There are many terrific books out there on investing and wealth building. Ann-Margaret understands it is not what you *make* but rather what you *keep* that matters. *Love and Money* goes that important step further and asks us to consider the folly of focusing exclusively on building wealth when it can be so easily lost to destructive breakups, lawsuits, sinister con artists, and ill-advised business dealings. She teaches us how to effectively utilize contracts for a variety of personal situations that could otherwise turn messy, and she also shows us how to erect legal barriers against those outside of our personal lives who may try to take advantage of us and destroy any wealth we may have accumulated. And she does so in language we can all understand, which is why she is such a valued expert contributor on *Dr. Phil*.

I have often said that money problems are not solved with money. There are powerful internal factors responsible for most lottery winners and other windfall recipients who blow through everything in short order. Ann-Margaret teaches us how to identify the traits within ourselves, such as low self-esteem, fear, and stress, which can negatively affect wealth. In *Love and Money*, she shares the actual internal strategies she utilized to go from being "in debt up to her eyeballs" to a successful real estate investor and business owner.

I highly recommend this book if you wish to protect your finances from costly legal and relationship troubles while simultaneously strengthening your financial bottom line. You will read this once and then continue to refer to it for years to come.

—Dr. Phil McGraw
November 2016

INTRODUCTION

Relationships with loved ones can dramatically impact our financial security. Our level of financial security, in turn, can profoundly alter the course of romantic and other relationships. The many intersections of love and wealth can produce explosive and potentially devastating legal consequences. Examining the effects of personal relationship fallouts on one's wealth has been largely uncharted territory in the realm of personal finance. Ignorance about the legal consequences of troubled relationships with loved ones, however, is the single biggest threat to one's wealth.

Broken hearts can be very expensive. We know that a contentious breakup can reduce our assets by half—not to mention the legal fees. Happy relationships can also cost us. This is because all relationships will eventually end. Our weakened state, in the wake of a loved one's death, can leave us vulnerable to con artists, greedy relatives, and inadvisable legal dealings.

What good is building up a nest egg if failed relationships and ill-advised legal dealings can wipe us out? The average American is far more likely to be involved in a costly legal dispute with a former loved one than with a stranger. Developing the ability to identify and avoid relationship landmines by implementing a few structures on the front end can prevent you from legally battling someone with whom you once shared Thanksgiving dinner (or a pillow).

The themes of love and money are inextricably intertwined. A problem with either of these areas can wreak havoc with the other. Conversely, getting a handle on either one of these areas will pay dividends in both. Improved relationships with loved ones can facilitate wealth building. A strong financial foundation, in turn, helps eliminate the single biggest source of relationship disputes—lack of money.

In terms of legal preparedness, an estimated 60 percent of American adults have gone through the exercise of creating a will. In the pages that follow, I will show how a will alone is incapable of protecting a family's wealth and relationships from today's unique challenges. A typical will utilizes a template that hasn't changed much in more than two hundred years. Often, only the names are changed, and the "new" document can be created in less time than it takes to boil water. This document, acting alone, fails miserably to adequately protect most families, and, moreover, is a pitiful last form of communication to our loved ones.

This book will introduce the love contract and other legal structures that are designed to protect wealth *for* us and our loved ones while also protecting wealth *from* our loved ones and their problems.

This is not a book about financial planning. Someone might be a financial genius and still lose more than half of his assets in a breakup because he wasn't legally protected. What does it matter whether our investment rate of return is 3, 4, 5, or 6 percent if we have a 40 to 50 percent chance of losing one-half of the assets to a bad breakup? Think the assets are safe if you are in a blissfully happy relationship? Not if you require extended long-term care or face other unexpected legal liabilities.

In the following pages, we will look at prenuptial, postnuptial, and cohabitation agreements, which have evolved in my law practice into a document I call the "love contract." We will examine the contract process itself and use it to deal with not only financial and legal problems but also love and relationship issues. Working with thousands of couples over the years, I have discovered that the contract process provides a unique and animus-free framework with which to resolve a wide variety of problems. Ultimately, the love contract can be used as a couple's personal mission statement.

We will explore external threats to our wealth in the form of con artists and toxic contracts as well as internal wealth impediments such as lack of personal vitality and low self-esteem.

Dozens of real-life cautionary tales will demonstrate how to prevent family feuds at death, how to properly protect our furry and feathered family members, and also how to prevent con artists from separating us from our wealth.

Last, through our love contract with the future, we present a tool with which to transmit ideas, values, and good deeds generations into the future. The love contract with the future allows us to protect and preserve our most important assets—those stored in our hearts and minds, for posterity.

1

PRENUPTIAL AGREEMENTS

When we think about contracts that protect assets, the document that pops into most minds is a prenuptial agreement. Nearly everyone has heard of "prenups," but the creation of one prior to getting married is still the exception rather than the rule.

My unscientific survey of the ten thousand clients I have worked with over the years indicates that fewer than 5 percent of them had prenuptial agreements prior to getting married. This makes sense in relation to older couples, as these agreements were virtually unheard of before the 1980s. After the 1980s, it became more common to read about celebrity couples and super high–net worth individuals getting prenups.

As an estate planning and asset protection attorney, I started to routinely offer prenuptial agreements to my clients as of the late 1990s. Wearing my "attorney hat," it makes perfect sense that we should do everything possible in order to protect ourselves against a costly divorce. This is, after all, the single biggest statistical threat to our net worth. Why, then, do most people giggle nervously when the subject is raised and proceed to jump headfirst into a legally unprotected marriage?

Think you don't need one? Neither did Sir Paul McCartney. That decision cost him an estimated $48.6 million—not including legal fees. Other celebrity examples abound. In a 2013 interview, the late Robin Williams described his most recent divorce as "having his heart ripped out through his wallet." He famously quipped that the term "alimony" was originally derived from the phrase "all the money." We see other legendary actors such as James Caan and Robert DeNiro bemoaning the "downstream" movie parts they feel forced to take in order to meet exorbitant alimony payments to exes. Throw some bad behavior into the mix, and there are truly no limits on the financial settlement that a judge can order. Tiger Woods's reported adultery is said to have cost him $100 million!

As a society, we are much more likely to take action to guard against other risks, even though they are statistically very remote when compared to the risk of divorce. Consider the fact that the overwhelming majority of us carry fire insurance on our homes. The actual risk of losing one's home to a fire is less than 1 percent.

The rational part of us knows that there is a 40 to 50 percent chance of divorce nationwide. However, nearly 100 percent of us entering marriage believe that we will be in the lucky one-half. It is clear that people about to be married are not coherently and objectively looking at these statistics. This reminds me of college freshman orientation. The moderator asked the auditorium of eighteen-year-olds who was going to graduate in the top 20 percent of the class. About 75 percent of the hands went up. We realized that more than half of us were wrong. Law school orientation presented more somber statistics. The dean of students began by telling us about all of the school's great athletic facilities, performing arts programs, and social events. He then deadpanned that it was a shame we would have no time for any of it, given the amount of work in store for us. Next, he asked us to look at the person to our right and then to our left. He seemed to take sadistic pleasure in announcing that one of the three of us would not make it to graduation day. As a class, our "attrition" or failure rate was only somewhat lower than the grim prediction. I am sure every student in that room believed they would complete the three-year law school program. More than 20 percent of them were wrong.

I suppose that our innate optimism protects us from self-identifying with any "failure" group. A little voice in our heads says, "My marriage will not be the one in two that doesn't make it, because I'm no quitter." The other reason that we don't internalize the 50 percent failure rate as a risk is that we are actually and quite literally "out of our minds" in the early stages of a relationship. It is impossible to imagine that you may, one day, be at odds with your beloved. There is strong brain chemistry at work during this initial euphoric phase. Scientists have described the oxytocin emitted during the early stage of a relationship as opiatelike and stronger than heroin. This can certainly alter one's objectivity and decision-making.

What I am asking you to do at this point is to read the rest of this chapter while, at the very least, considering the possibility (however remote that may seem to your besotted mind) that you may not be objectively analyzing your exposure to risk at this point in time.

Even if you remain unable to imagine your partner ever changing or acting in a less than honorable fashion, then consider the possibility that you may change. Much of the work we do in estate planning centers on the possibility that we may undergo physical or mental changes as time progresses. We must erect legal guardrails in the form of advance directives and trusts so that we are protected from possible evildoers and other external threats as well as our own folly. A prenup should really be viewed as an extension of your estate planning protections, designed to shield both of you from changes in behavior either of you may exhibit in the future.

If you feel like you are courting doom by discussing endgame rules on the front end, please remember that these rules already exist. By getting married, you are entering into a contract. There are more than one thousand rights, rules, and responsibilities that flow from the legal marriage contract. Exit rules are already in place. The problem is that they were written by someone else. As a former state legislator, I worked with my colleagues to try to come up with "default" laws to govern many areas of life that an individual fails to plan for. A common example of such a default rule is when someone dies without a will. Every state has an inheritance formula to distribute our stuff upon death. These "statutory" beneficiaries may or may not be the folks whom I wanted to inherit my assets.

Relying on your state's default property distribution rules upon divorce is especially problematic, because there is a stranger in the mix. The judge (some are strange, indeed) is charged with interpreting and applying the default rules that other strangers (your state legislators) voted into law. Most states are so-called "equitable distributions" as opposed to community property jurisdictions. This means that the judge is given pretty wide latitude to ensure that "equity" is achieved. This is a sort of fuzzy and decidedly subjective mission, which can produce some absurd results.

If you feel that the rules, or the judge's application of them, are unfair, you will likely fight them through your lawyer. He or she is yet another stranger in the mix. You will pay him or her handsomely to fight against someone else's rules and decisions.

Engaged couples are prepared to customize many aspects of the wedding celebration and vows. You wouldn't say to your caterer or bridal seamstress, "I'll take whatever most people have." This is your future, and you can and should customize it so that it pleases you. It is in this spirit that I implore you to not allow a bunch of strangers to script your marriage endgame and future security if, for whatever reason, the marriage doesn't work. Customize your rules ahead of time.

I think that the most natural way to contemplate a prenuptial agreement is in the context of our other estate planning discussions. Remember that all marriages will end—either at death or through divorce. We readily engage in estate planning to ensure that a surviving spouse has as smooth and financially secure a transition as possible. It is in this spirit that we should create documents to ensure that neither one of us will ever be subjected to strangers' strange rules in the event that the marriage doesn't work out. Think of the prenup as a way to protect both of you. It is a way of saying to your partner, "I love you and want to spend my life with you. However, if, for any unforeseeable reason, 'we' don't work, either permanently or temporarily, it is important to me that we make certain promises to each other as a tribute to the love that we now share. Let's take steps to ensure that each of us will always be as financially stable as possible. I also want for us to promise that we will always treat each other with respect and never publicly speak negatively about the other."

The Contract Process

The themes of love, protection, and respect should form the underpinnings of your prenuptial agreement. It can and should also deal with far more than simply who gets what in the endgame. This is why I began using the term "love contract" for prenups that contain any provisions in addition to a bare-bones property distribution. As you will see in the pages ahead, there is really no limit to the degree of creativity or personalization you can have within a love contract. At its essence are the enduring themes of protection and respect. Contrary to popular belief, we are not simply focused on the wealthier party protecting her assets from the other. Instead, any good contract begins with each party deciding what they want in a given venture and then determining what they are willing and unwilling to do or give in order to reach the goal. In determining our limits, we seek to protect ourselves from all "knowable risks." These risks encompass far more than merely financial issues. Both parties always have a lot at stake—regardless of whether or not they have any assets to speak of. They should, therefore, be full partners in the contracting process. The process begins by each party separately considering the following.

1. WHAT DO I WANT?

We begin by determining what it is that we truly want. First, we think about what kind of relationship we want. Here, we consider aspirational items, which comprise the "mission statement" portion of the love contract (see chapter 12). We must then think about what we want in the context of a possible breakup. For starters, this should include a peaceful "endgame." Next, what would we need, financially, in order to be on solid footing in the event of a breakup? To assess this, you will need to consider many factors. Is a geographic move or career disruption contemplated in advance of the marriage? Will you be living in a house or apartment owned by the other party? If so, what will the short-term and long-term living arrangements be upon breakup (or death)? If you are the partner with more money, this question will cause you to determine your "firewall." This is the number below which you cannot comfortably exist. This is your baseline security amount. You do not gamble with this, you don't give it to your cousin to invest, and you do not leave it on the table going into a marriage and simply hope for the best. This would be reckless. Think of it this way: if you didn't insure the integrity of this baseline amount, your psychological security would be undermined. You probably wouldn't be very pleasant to be around. So, you aren't doing anyone any favors by not protecting yourself first.

This initial self-assessment phase should also cause you to take inventory of any past relationship ghosts. Yes, it is usually in poor taste to regale your partner with tales of past romances. However, if you have any "hot buttons" that are a result of weird, annoying, or damaging past relationships, it is important to "contract against them" here. My clients have no shortage of cautionary tales that they are determined to avoid the "next time around."

FRANK'S STORY

My client Frank's former mother-in-law always accompanied him and his now ex-wife on vacation. Whether it was a three-day weekend in the country or a two-week "dream vacation" in Hawaii, Mama was there, in her orthopedic shoes and floppy hat. Frank tried telling his wife that he craved time alone with her. She was sympathetic but felt conflicted because her mother was a widow with health issues and really enjoyed the getaways. The couple also had a host of other problems and eventually called it quits. It was the group vacations, though, that haunted him and caused him to vow that he would never marry again. When I told him and his current girlfriend that they could deal with this issue within a prenup, it seemed to lighten the load of some of his baggage. His girlfriend readily agreed to solo vacations and also had a few requests of her own. Her last boyfriend was a TV sports junkie and spent the better part of every evening and weekend in front of the TV. This annoyed her to the point of being sick over it. She was intrigued to learn that she could address this issue within a prenup and thereby avoid having to be a "sports widow" ever again.

By focusing on our own needs first, we can avoid the trap of being too "giving" on the front end. I have often seen a partner say, "I am not marrying you for your money. To prove it, I will sign whatever you want." Sometimes the partner with fewer assets wants to show the other (and his family!) that her intentions are pure. When I hear this, I actually yell at my clients: "You aren't doing anyone any favors by signing a one-sided contract in martyr-like fashion!" The implication of doing so is that you don't have any assets or anything else of value that merits legal protection. This is not the right tone to set at the beginning of what should be a loving and mutually supportive and respectful partnership. By signing "whatever the other one wants," you are not being respectful of yourself. By extension, as mothers have told daughters for eons, "how do you expect anyone else to respect you if you don't respect yourself?" Remember the airplane metaphor: put your oxygen mask on first. Otherwise you will be useless to everyone around you.

The party with fewer assets must start by considering what he needs in order to be made whole in the event of a breakup. I consider three months of living expense money to be the absolute minimum. From here, it is advisable to project out how your needs may change in years to come. If, for example, you have been out of the workforce for five years because of the marriage, you may need to hone career skills by going back to school or relocating in order to find your next job. This will require greater financial resources.

The bottom line with step one is to avoid one-sided contracts. They are mean-spirited and can be challenged later on by a party claiming that they were coerced into signing. All contracts rest on a firmer foundation when both parties receive something of value from it.

2. WHAT CAN I GIVE? WHAT ARE MY LIMITS?

Once we have established what we want, we can move on to the second step in the contracting process: What am I able to do and give in order to achieve my goal? Just as important, we need to determine our limits. In this step, the party with more money should consider what she can comfortably give to the other in the event of a breakup. Just as important, she needs to determine her financial firewall—this is the amount she is unwilling to lose. Ideally, the amount that can comfortably be paid out will bear some resemblance to the figure arrived at by your partner in step one.

Beyond the baseline financial issues, we next need to consider what else we can promise the other. Your wedding vows will include a blanket pledge to "love, honor, and cherish." Step two of the love contracting process should cause you to put some flesh on these wedding vow bones. In other words, what are some concrete ways that I can love and honor my partner?

I recommend that couples begin step two by promising never to publicly malign the other. This should apply not only in the event of a breakup but also during the intact relationship. We all know that there will be some disagreements and problems ahead in any relationship. By promising not to speak ill of the other in public, we seek to establish civilized and respectful "rules of engagement." No one likes to be publicly embarrassed. I have had a few divorced clients tell me that they knew the marriage was over when their spouse made disparaging remarks about them in front of other people.

Why should we want to put something as basic as this in writing? Because in the heat of anger, respectful conduct does not always "come naturally."

LARRY AND SUE'S STORY

The "no maligning the other" clause was initially inspired by my client Larry. He was a self-made and highly successful business owner who grew up in poverty. His wife, Sue, grew up in a comfortable upper-middle-income environment. Larry told me about going to a dinner party with Sue. A colleague, who had had "one too many" ribbed Larry about wearing a suit to the more "casual chic" get-together. In an unthinking attempt to deflect the barb with humor, Sue told the group that Larry grew up in a trailer park and can't be expected to always get the details quite right. Yes, this was a thoughtless and insensitive comment. For Larry, though, it cut him to the quick. He told me that he felt reduced to his inner "poor kid" who could never quite measure up. He had simultaneous feelings of mortification and hatred toward Sue. This stupid comment was the beginning of their end.

When promising not to publicly malign your partner, you should take special note about what their personal sore spots may be. In Larry's case, it should have been obvious to Sue that he would never be completely over the difficult and often embarrassing circumstances of his poor childhood. By making a mental list of your partner's likely "sore spots," you can avoid unnecessarily hurting him during an argument or in front of others. Note that this sore-spot list should be made and kept mentally. Putting this list in writing or announcing it would be very insulting. Imagine your partner's reaction if you were to proudly proclaim that you will never intentionally embarrass him on account of being fat, bald, short, etc.

The "no maligning" promise in the context of a love contract takes the form of a "nondisclosure" clause. This is almost always a part of a celebrity or high-profile couple's prenup. The essence of this clause is that you promise not to pen a "tell all" book or do the talk-show circuit sharing your celeb ex's weird fetishes. This provision comes with built-in carrot and stick financial features. When you see a tight-lipped divorcing party emerge from court, shielded by her smirking attorney, who barks a clipped "no comment" to the paparazzi, you can be sure that she is complying with such a nondisclosure clause.

3. NEGOTIATE AND COLLABORATE

Step three of the contracting process causes you to imagine what the two of you, as a couple, can accomplish and create together. At the heart of any collaborative legal endeavor is the notion that what you can be, make, and do together is greater than the arithmetic sum of what you can be, make, and do separately. This step forms the basis of your mission statement. It is central to all of the love contracts (prenups, postnups, and cohabs). The mission statement is the prenup's higher ground. This is covered in chapter 12.

Prenup FAQs

Q. My son is engaged. How can I convince him to get a prenup?

A. You can't. The thought of an evil ex-in-law getting a hold of your child's assets one day may keep you up at night. But if your child refuses to agree to a prenup, this is his or her prerogative as an adult. Rather than completely dropping the issue, though, consider a more limited approach. If your daughter is adamant about keeping her "love blinders" firmly in place and wishes to cast her lot together with Mr. Wonderful, you will need to acknowledge to her that this is ultimately her decision. However, do you not have a right to ask your child to consider a limited prenuptial agreement as it relates to your assets currently earmarked for your child in your will? Yes, I know you heard that inherited assets are off limits in a divorce settlement. That is what we refer to in law school as "Black Letter Law." It is true. If asked on a game show, the correct answer is that inherited assets don't get split. However, in the real world, there are many ways that inherited assets can and do get split between the parties in a divorce.

If your son inherits a brokerage account and puts his wife's name on it, guess who will get it in the event of a split. What about the vacation property that you willed to your daughter alone? Well, if your son-in-law planted a rosebush or fixed a broken curtain rod on the property, he will likely claim his "fair" share upon breakup. He will claim that his efforts were essential to the preservation of the property (puhleez!).

Even if your child is scrupulous about keeping assets off limits and totally separate from a spouse, they may still be unsafe. If, for example, one party has a $50,000 money market account that was inherited from Grandma, a judge is technically not able to order that it be split. However, he or she may give the other party more of another asset to even up the sides.

The themes of love contracting and estate planning often intersect and can never be viewed entirely separately. In the context of parents' estate planning, I have seen courts consider a child's future interest in a trust as countable when distributing the couple's assets. This was so even though the creator of the trust was still alive and the child would not actually receive anything until the parent's death.

Q. My business partner has fallen madly in love with someone she just met online. Do I have a legal right to request that she get a prenup?

A. That depends on the terms of your partnership, shareholder, or LLC operating agreement. I always encourage my clients to include a love contract provision within their corporate governance documents. This would require all partners to agree to create a prenup, postnup, or cohab depending on their relationship status. This provision clearly spells out that the business entity is separate property not to be considered in any postbreakup financial division. Without this requirement, your partner's failed romance will become your business headache. The business will be subjected to a full-blown valuation. You can expect forensic accountants to be swarming around your workplace. Your personal tax returns could even be subpoenaed in order to determine whether all of the divorcing party's income and assets are being accounted for. Having this legal protection in place will prevent anyone from ever having to liquidate his or her business interests in a fire-sale manner in order to raise cash for a costly divorce settlement. It will also prevent you from having a stranger as your new partner.

Q. I have heard of prenuptial agreements not being enforced. Why bother getting one?

A. The short answer is that any overturned prenup must not have been properly made in the first place. The more apt question would be, "How do I ensure that my prenup will be enforced later?" Having reviewed all of the cases where a prenup was stricken down, we can isolate three poison pills, which, if avoided, should ensure that yours will stand:

1. Both parties should have separate counsel. This is not an area where you want to economize. If you share a lawyer or go it alone without a lawyer, you may as well not bother with the agreement. The classic way out of a prenup is to claim that one was not given the opportunity to have the terms reviewed and explained by independent counsel. Counsel for one party should not even recommend an attorney for the other side.

2. Never sign the prenup immediately before the marriage. If a prenup were signed the day before the wedding, then the

party who wishes to get out of it would have an excellent argument that they signed "under duress." What constitutes a safe proximity before the wedding? Several months is ideal. If you have a shorter time frame and don't wish to postpone the wedding, then sign the prenup but consider bolstering it with an identically termed postnuptial agreement created after the wedding (more on this in chapter 2).

3. Include an accurate itemized list of your assets. Failure to disclose all of your assets can provide the other party with an effective argument that he or she was not aware of the true extent of the property interests being waived. Avoid blanket descriptions, such as "all of my assets." This could be challenged. It is also advisable to provide copies of the three most recently filed federal income tax returns.

4. Be honest about your assets and also about your debts. It is not pleasant to have a lot of debt, not to mention having to disclose this fact to your loved one. However, if you don't give a full disclosure of your weak financial position in the prenup, you will be at a clear disadvantage in a future possible property settlement. It won't look very good for you to explain to the judge that you need more financial help from the other party than is readily apparent, because you fibbed in the prenuptial agreement (which you had to swear to before a notary). The same holds true for inflating the value of assets you list. Pride has a place in the first step of this contracting process but not in the disclosure step. I have seen the "poorer" party estimate that her grandmother's cameo is worth many thousands of dollars. This is a silly attempt to appear to be more financially solvent than is accurate. I understand the impulse, but please resist doing this. Again, you will be in a bad position when and if it is ever time to distribute assets. You will likely get $10,000 less if you pretended you had an asset of that value in the prenup.

Q. *Isn't a prenup unromantic?*
A. No—think of it as an extension of one's wedding vows. Ideally, it can be a joint goal-setting exercise that covers so much more

than just money. What's not romantic is letting some strange judge decide who gets your stuff (and pets!) in the event of a divorce.

Q. Why can't we just make verbal promises to each other?

A. Putting something in writing guards against faulty expectations and faulty recollections. When something is important, we put it in writing (e.g., to-do lists, New Year's resolutions, etc.). Research shows that we are more likely to remember and prioritize things if we write them down.

Q. A prenup is only important for the wealthy party, right?

A. Not if it is correctly prepared. A prenup should make sure that both spouses are in a decent financial position if the marriage doesn't work out. This is especially true if one partner is planning to postpone or sacrifice career-advancement opportunities for the sake of the marriage.

Q. Isn't it awkward to bring it up?

A. I tell my clients to blame it on their parents or on me. If there is a family business involved, the corporate rules should require all shareholders to enter into prenups (or postnups or cohabs) to avoid forced liquidation if any family members divorce. Blaming it on the lawyer is easy—no one likes us anyway!

Q. What are some of the lifestyle clauses that couples are incorporating into their prenups?

A. I advise my clients to start by looking at failed relationships they've had and isolating their "poison pill" items. Some couples have negotiated limits on clothes spending, cosmetic surgery obsessions, and sexual bucket list items as well as weight-gain penalties.

2

POSTNUPTIAL AGREEMENTS

For generations, spouses who had issues to resolve only had two choices: grin and bear it or leave. This is because legal contracts between married people were not recognized under common law. Today, married couples in forty-six states have the right to contract with each other in order to resolve or prevent a whole host of problems. Increased legal acceptance has resulted in matrimonial attorneys drafting more of these agreements than ever before.

Postnuptial agreements can be used to settle a wide variety of marital disputes. Financial disagreements, housekeeping issues, and vacation selections are common components of these contracts. Some couples even ask to include a "sex schedule" within the document. You will be glad to know that this schedule would not be legally enforceable in a court of law. However, it may still be useful in order to clarify expectations between the parties. See more on the "life style" clauses in chapter 12.

Postnuptial agreements can be used to strengthen a prenup that was entered into too close to the wedding day. Most often, though, they are used in times of marital crisis. When the cheating spouse is groveling for a second chance, the aggrieved party can now ask for more than just his or her word that it won't happen again. Monetary penalties for future indiscretions are commonly incorporated into the document.

KEN AND LOUISE'S STORY

"Ken" and "Louise" were referred to me to discuss a possible postnup in the wake of his infidelity. Louise was truly on the verge of leaving and grappled with very mixed emotions regarding their future. A trip to a marriage counselor provided little help. The counselor basically told Louise that it was her decision as to whether she should stay or leave. However, if she chose to stay, it would not be "constructive" to continually bring up "the incident." At my conference table, Ken promised Louise that it would never happen again. He "now realized just how important [she] was to him" and that "this chapter could somehow ultimately result in a stronger and better relationship." I was proud of my self-restraint in not rolling my eyes when Ken said this. Instead, I asked if he was willing to agree to a penalty provision within the postnup. (Justin Timberlake and Michael Douglas are both reported to have agreed to such infidelity clauses.) The gist of Ken and Louise's clause was that if either party was unfaithful at any time, and a divorce occurred thereafter, then the aggrieved party would receive 60 percent of all assets.

Ken agreed to the penalty provision. He had it reviewed by a separate attorney, and they both signed. Two years passed, and things improved between them. For Ken's fiftieth birthday, he asked Louise if she would possibly agree to a threesome. This was his biggest "bucket list" item. Her initial reluctance was short-lived. Louise was an enthusiastic participant and ultimately developed a relationship with the other woman. Louise eventually left Ken to marry Renee. Ken was devastated. During the divorce, Ken's lawyer tried to enforce the 60 percent penalty clause within the postnup. This didn't work in Ken's favor, however, because he "consented" to the initial relationship with Renee. It therefore did not qualify as "infidelity" as defined by the contract. In fact, the only conduct that qualified as infidelity was Ken's original affair. Because the divorce took place after the original episode (the agreement did not require that the divorce immediately follow the infidelity), Louise ended up with 60 percent of the couple's assets. I advised her to create a prenup before taking the plunge with Renee.

Postnuptial Agreements for the Happily Married

I encourage all of my married clients to consider creating a postnup. This comes as a surprise to nearly everyone I suggest it to. Why on earth would a happily married couple need a postnup? *Because without one, your entire estate plan might unravel.*

VIVIAN AND CARLOS'S STORY

Vivian and Carlos created wills with me more than
ten years ago. Their "distribution scheme" within the
wills was what you might imagine. Upon the death of
the first spouse, they each wanted all of the assets
to pass to the survivor. Then, upon the death of the
surviving spouse, they wanted their assets to be distributed equally to their two children, Carlos Jr. and
Tina-Marie. Their biggest concern was that they did
not want any assets passing "outside of the family"
to either of their children's spouses. Instead, they
wanted the assets to go from their children directly
to grandchildren. They gave me strict instructions
that "nothing goes to the in-laws!"

I explained to them that once their children inherited the assets, they were legally free to do with
them as they pleased. This included sharing the assets
with their spouses. Vivian and Carlos were adamant
about preventing any of their wealth from going to the
in-laws. They were only barely on speaking terms with
their son-in-law, Vinny. They hadn't spoken at all to
their daughter-in-law, Tanya, in five years. Having
prepared wills for twenty years, I have come to learn
that it is very common for my clients to have issues
with their children's spouses. Five years without
speaking, though, was pretty severe. What could have
caused this? I felt that it was my job to ask. Somewhat ironically, it turned out that the feud erupted
over an estate planning discussion. Shortly after the
birth of their first grandchild, Vivian and Carlos
suggested that Carlos Jr. and Tanya create wills to
name guardians for little Joachim. Tanya informed them
that they already created a will shortly before Joachim was born. The will named *her* parents as the legal

guardians of little Joachim in the event that she and Carlos Jr. were to die before his eighteenth birthday. Vivian was devastated! How could Carlos Jr. have gone along with this? Tanya's parents were so clearly unfit. They practiced a "bizarre" religion and were so utterly ignorant that Vivian felt that it should be against the law for them to even vote.

In response to my further questioning, Vivian conceded that she was still on speaking terms with her son. Yes, she was hurt that he agreed to the selection of his wife's parents, but Vivian reasoned that Tanya must have pressured him into it. "Surely he was subjected to that domineering *%#!*'s control," Vivian hissed. I turned to Carlos, and as if on cue, he dutifully nodded his silent assent.

I again explained that they couldn't prevent Carlos Jr. from sharing his ultimate inheritance with Tanya. That is, unless they (Vivian) felt strongly enough that they were willing to legally restrict Carlos Jr.'s access to his one-half of the estate. And so it was that Vivian instructed me to draft each of their wills as follows: Upon the death of the first spouse, everything goes to the survivor. Upon the second death, whatever is left of the estate goes one-half to Tina-Marie and one-half into a trust for Carlos Jr.'s limited lifetime benefit. Their financial advisor, Shari, was named as the Trustee for Carlos Jr. The trust dictated that she give him 5 percent of the trust assets each year, and then upon his death, anything left in his trust was to go to Joachim, together with any future possible siblings he may have.

While this might not be the solution most people would come up with, it was clearly what Vivian wanted. She and Carlos definitely took my advice to customize their estate planning based on their individual situation.

One year after the wills were signed, Vivian died in a car accident. I heard that Carlos was in a state of shock. I called and suggested that he come into the office to review his legal planning. He said that he would but never did.

Five years later, Tina-Marie and Carlos Jr. made an appointment with me after their father died. I assumed that the meeting was to discuss probating the will we had drafted years earlier. I was wrong. They showed me a photocopy of a newer will in which Carlos left everything to Shari. "His financial advisor?" I asked. "And widow" Tina-Marie added. Tina-Marie and Carlos Jr. would have only received the estate if Shari had died first. Given the fact that she was eighteen years younger than Carlos, this was never a very likely scenario.

I thought about Vivian and how fervently she wished for the family's assets to remain with her children and grandchildren. Now, everything was in the hands of a stranger to the family and there was nothing that could be done to correct it.

I thought hard about what went wrong here. I had reached out to Carlos when I heard about Vivian's death. If he had come in, I definitely would have urged him to get a prenup in the event of a subsequent remarriage. I then concluded that Shari could have easily talked him out of doing one, even if I did have a chance to recommend it. I thought back to my meetings with Vivian and Carlos and how she set the agenda and Carlos just seemed to acquiesce to her wishes.

Carlos and Vivian's story forced me to think about my own husband and what would happen to our assets in the event that he survived me. What good is a well-constructed estate plan if a weak-willed surviving spouse can turn it on its head? It was then that I began suggesting to my clients that all estate plans should include a limited postnuptial agreement. This requires each party to agree that they will enter into a prenuptial agreement prior to any future possible remarriage. My husband, Bill, and I were my first clients. Now, I don't have to worry about another woman talking him out of getting a prenup if he survives me. He doesn't have to have a backbone! He can simply blame it on poor old dead me for making him legally commit in advance to doing one.

Using a Postnup to Resolve Financial Problems

Financial difficulties and disagreements have long been among the top factors driving couples to breakup. Remember Billy Joel's friends "Brenda and Eddie" who "started to fight when the money got tight, and they just didn't count on the tears"? Perhaps it was the ill-advised "big water bed that they bought with the bread they had saved for a couple of years" that set them on an unstable financial road. Today's young couples are even more likely to be suffering from some degree of financial stress. There are many reasons for this. The cost of higher education has exploded in the past twenty years. Young people are borrowing dizzying amounts of money to pay for college degrees. Today's job market, however, does not guarantee that all of the newly minted grads will find gainful employment. In fact, there are more unemployed college graduates today than there are job openings requiring a college degree. The near impossibility of paying off the average student debt of $25,000 when unemployed or underemployed becomes painfully obvious six months after leaving school when the first student loan bills come in. Add credit card debt to this mix (the average cardholder has a balance of $8,000), and we have the fault lines of a financial disaster waiting to happen. This is the unstable foundation on which newlyweds are beginning their financial lives together.

The single most important thing that we can do to prevent marital money woes on the front end is to avoid a wedding ceremony beyond our means. According to a 2015 survey of 13,000 couples by Theknot.com, the average cost of a wedding in the United States is $30,000! This is two-thirds of what the average college graduate (who is lucky enough to be able to find a job) can expect to make in a whole year. Incurring expenses that you cannot comfortably afford will make you feel icky. When all of these bills start rolling in after the honeymoon, you may end up resenting each other. There is an old saying: "If money is a problem, then everything else is a problem."

The postnup can provide a framework and a mechanism to wrestle your financial demons into submission as a team. The postnup process employs the same three-step contracting process introduced in chapter 1.

1. WHAT DO I WANT AND NEED?

The first step in the contracting process requires us to look inward. Here, we assess our personal long-term financial needs and goals. Do I wish to be debt free? Do I wish to create a financial cushion to allow me to quit my current job and start a dream business? Where do I see myself financially in five years?

2. WHAT CAN I GIVE? WHAT ARE MY LIMITS?

In the second step of the process, each partner separately assesses what he or she can give, or in this case give up, in order to move toward the goals identified in the first step. Knowing that the rest of the process will require some immediate belt-tightening, you should list a few current nonnegotiable expense items. Yes, we all know about the magical long-term wealth-creating properties of saying no to your fancy take-out coffee. But if an occasional mocha-cho-ca-whatever makes you happy, then I believe this should be on your nonnegotiable list. I don't think it is constructive at this juncture to focus on your partner's wayward money behaviors. Instead, ask yourself what you, alone, can do to achieve the wants and needs outlined in step one. This requires a critical and unvarnished look at your own overspending. As an estate attorney, I am always amazed by people's "money stories." In terms of generating wealth, what you earn truly matters less than what you save. I see physician and attorney clients who are mired in debt while many of their "blue collar" counterparts retire with millions. No matter what we earn, all of us have spending areas that can be reined in. You may be able to drastically slash the grocery bill, for example, by leaving your kids at home when you shop. The amount saved will more than cover the cost of a sitter. Ask any mother if you need this concept explained. Reduce the magazine subscriptions; eat at home more. You know what to do. Buy fewer items of better quality that can be repaired as needed, as opposed to being discarded. Become a master of delayed gratification. Every discretionary purchase that is put off will free up more "goal money" now.

3. NEGOTIATE AND COLLABORATE

The third step in the financial love contracting process requires you to sit down with your partner and compare notes. Share your goals and needs identified in step one. Then reveal what you are each willing to cut back on in order to get there. How much will this free up? How do you wish to direct this money stream (or trickle)? Some financial gurus suggest that you use all of it to pay down debt. I agree that it is always a good idea to pay down debt. Compare the interest rate on your unpaid balances with the corresponding rate of interest a bank would pay you to deposit this money into savings. However, there is a powerful force at work when you see a savings balance begin to grow. I don't want people to be deprived of this motivational force until the debt is totally wiped out. Therefore, I recommend a hybrid approach. Start paying down some debt at the same time that you start your savings habit. It is OK if the amounts allocated to each goal are pitiful at first. The tiniest steps in the right direction are moving us in that direction and can generate momentum if kept up over time.

The fun and powerful part of this step is when you engage in some joint goal setting. What will you direct your finances toward when the debt is wiped out? Will one or both of you start a sideline business? Will you donate to your house of worship or favorite charity?

The love contracting process works well to solve financial problems for several reasons. First, by starting with our own wants and needs, we ensure that we don't bend too far initially, thereby endangering the entire process. Next, by setting goals down on paper, we are far more likely to remember them and stick to them than if the same goals were merely articulated in conversation. Throughout the process, by specifically avoiding pointing fingers at each other's perceived financial mistakes, we are taking away the animus factor. Instead, our focus remains on the one area we are most likely able to control—our own behavior. Remember, you can't change someone else. Attempts to do so will meet with failure while serving only to frustrate both of you. Your positive approach cannot help but inspire your partner to engage in similar responsible behavior. Collaborative goal setting, which is the third step in this process, is a proven method of turbocharging your results. Corporate leaders have long known that the most effective way to achieve any goal is to assemble a team to focus on it. Positive teamwork can achieve results greater than the arithmetic sum of what is possible from the individual participants. By removing the finger pointing and criticism, both team members are freed up to focus on mutual support and the creative process. This process can be applied to any common sources of marital strife!

Test Your Postnup IQ

1. *True or false: My husband asked me to sign a postnuptial agreement. This means he wants a divorce.* Probably false. Now that all states have so-called "No Fault Divorce," either party can opt out of a marriage at any time. However, sometimes a party tries to hammer out a favorable property division within a postnup prior to filing for divorce. Depending upon the timing between the postnup and the divorce filing, this could invalidate the postnup on the grounds of fraudulent inducement.

2. *We are on a tight budget. Can we share an attorney?* No. Postnuptial agreements have been invalidated by courts when

both parties were not independently represented by counsel of their own choosing. A better way to keep costs down is for each party to come up with a list of their marital problems as well as proposed compromise solutions prior to meeting with the attorney. This can greatly reduce the dreaded "billable hours."

3. *True or false: A postnuptial agreement only benefits the wealthy spouse.* False. A good postnuptial agreement should protect both spouses. A postnup that is completely one-sided will probably be invalidated by the court. If, for example, one party put his or her career on hold or turned down out-of-state promotion opportunities for the sake of the marriage, these are factors that should be addressed within the postnup. Ideally, this document will ensure the financial security of both spouses in the event that the hoped-for reconciliation does not work out.

4. *True or false: Happily married couples don't need a postnup.* False! I encourage all of my estate planning clients to create postnups. Even if a marriage defies the statistical divorce perils, it will end at death. I have seen way too many widows and widowers lose their assets to ill-advised marriages entered into while they were still grieving the loss of their first spouse. Within a postnup, each spouse can promise to enter into a prenuptial agreement prior to any possible future remarriage in order to protect the assets from the first marriage. This protects not only the children of the first marriage but also the surviving spouse from being taken advantage of by mercenary characters.

5. *True or false: A postnup can prevent fights over money.* True. We all know that finances are a leading cause of all breakups. I have found that when couples address spending expectations and financial goals proactively, they can avoid unspoken and simmering tensions that tend to erupt into a lot of fighting.

6. *True or false: A postnuptial agreement only deals with financial issues.* False. A postnup provides a contractual framework to deal with any and all sources of conflict and unfulfillment.

Lifestyle clauses dealing with overspending, gambling, weight gain, substance abuse issues, infidelity, TV time, and social media parameters can be addressed within a postnup. This is why I like to think of a postnuptial agreement as a couple's mission statement or love contract.

3

COHABITATION AGREEMENTS

Many people will remember the famous 1977 case of *Marvin v. Marvin*, when Michelle Triola sued actor Lee Marvin for support after they had lived together unmarried for several years. The case was a media sensation and made the term "palimony" part of the American lexicon. In the end, Triola was unable to prove that a contract—written or verbal—existed between herself and the Academy Award–winning actor, meaning she had no claim to Marvin's considerable assets. The case, however, paved the way for being able to collect against a live-in love interest.

Unmarried couples sharing a household should definitely consider creating a cohabitation type of love contract that sets forth certain ground rules. The "cohab" should deal with the couple's expectations during the relationship as well as the division of property upon breakup. The breakup of an unmarried couple can have more than a few wrinkles not found in divorce cases.

TERRI AND ED'S STORY

Terri and Ed dated on and off for two years following Ed's bitter divorce. He did not unequivocally rule out marriage, but he made it clear that it would be a long way down the road. Terri was undaunted. She was sure that if she put the time in and remained patient, Ed would come around. When Terri's apartment lease renewal contained a 20 percent rent hike, she asked Ed if she could crash at his place, just while she looked for another apartment. Once in his home, Terri lost no time making herself indispensable. She bought groceries, cleaned, and even cooked occasionally. Terri's new apartment never did materialize. They fell into a comfortable rhythm, punctuated by Terri's occasional marriage references. One year after moving in, Terri intensified her focus. She told Ed that her Aunt Fran had been diagnosed with macular degeneration. Terri was heartsick that she would be the only woman in her family for whom Aunt Fran would not be able to hand sew a custom wedding gown—that is, unless Ed wouldn't think that it was totally bizarre to have Fran create one for Terri now, before she lost her vision. She joked with Ed that the ultimate wedding might not even feature him, so he shouldn't feel any pressure.

The gown was a masterpiece. Terri showed it to all of their friends, who began asking Ed when they were going to set a date. Though he hadn't technically popped the question yet, Ed seemed to be objecting less to her marriage "program." Over dinner one night, Terri revealed ten index cards with the words

"Honeymoon Destination" written across the top. Just for fun, she suggested that they each write their top five destinations and then trade cards to see if there were any matches. Bingo! They each selected Sicily. Though there was still no date (or proposal) in sight, Terri treasured the "Honeymoon" index card with Ed's writing on it.

Convinced that he really wanted her to take the initiative, Terri proceeded to sign up for a bridal registry. When Ed received the confirmation and con- gratulatory email from the store, he lost it. He imme- diately began packing up her belongings and putting the boxed items in the hallway. When Terri and her sister Sharon got home from the mall, Ed told her that he'd had it. Her bizarre little fantasy had succeeded in taking their relationship to an entirely different level, all right. They were now over! Loud enough for the neighbors to hear, Ed yelled that Terri needed psychological help and he would not marry her. His neighbor, Suzy, opened her door to see Ed throw the wedding gown at Terri.

In spite of her broken heart, Terri was determined not to let him get away with treating her so horri- bly. She met with four separate attorneys who told her that there was no legal remedy available to her. Undaunted as always, Terri's fifth consultation landed her an attorney who took the case on a contingency fee basis. They proceeded to sue Ed for "Breach of Prom- ise to Marry." Ed had a good laugh when he was served with process. The smile was long gone by the time his attorney told him that his was one of twenty-six states that still had these laws on the books. "But I never even proposed to her," railed Ed. After listen- ing to the entire twisted tale, Ed's attorney asked him what the jury would think once they heard that Ed

had driven Terri to multiple wedding dress fittings?
What about the card, in his writing, selecting their
honeymoon destination? What about neighbors who could
testify to hearing him "call off the wedding"? Ed
could take his chances with a sympathetic jury, or he
could offer Terri $50,000 to drop the case. He paid
the $50,000, consoling himself with the (incorrect)
notion that he would be able to deduct this payment
from his income taxes that year as a gambling loss.

The moral of Ed and Terri's cautionary tale is that you can never underestimate the sympathy factor when juries are asked to compensate the lovelorn. Law students learn about the sympathy factor from studying court battles like the 2008 Georgia case of *Shell v. Gibbs*. The testimony in this case revealed that Wayne Gibbs had given his fiancée, Rosemary Shell, $30,000 to bail her out of credit card debt. When he learned that she really had way more debt than this, he soured on the relationship. He decided to end their engagement. Perhaps, in retrospect, he may have chosen a kinder method than a note left for her in the bathroom. She promptly sued him for $150,000—and won!

These cases illustrate the importance of setting forth the parties' understanding regarding the possibility of marriage. This is especially important if one of the parties does not intend to be married at any point. This will prevent a party from later claiming that he was misled or that he believed the cohabitation would lead to marriage and was somehow duped into "wasting" precious years in the relationship. Even with the clause in place, I urge my clients who don't wish to get married to be very careful when choosing gifts of jewelry—nothing round, please!

The "Marriage Position Clause" can also immunize the parties from a common-law marriage claim. A century ago, every state accorded legal marital status to cohabiting couples who "held themselves out" as married. Even though most states have done away with common-law marriage, I have had several clients' estates sued for the one-third marital elective share by the surviving nonspouse partner. On what grounds, you ask? In all of the cases, the unmarried couple traveled to a jurisdiction that still has common-law marriage (Washington, DC, for example) and checked into a hotel as "Mr. and Mrs." This quaint and seemingly harmless gesture left the decedent's estate subject to a challenge that the couple "held themselves out as married" in a jurisdiction where common-law marriage is legal. The home state could then be required to acknowledge this "marriage" by virtue of the US Constitution's "Full Faith and Credit" provision.

One of the tricky issues in creating a cohab can be deciding upon what constitutes living together. This is plainly obvious when one or both parties leaves their current abode and a moving van is involved. In reality, though, many people retain separate homes. Is it living together when the couple spends two nights per week together? Three? Four? The answer is trickier still with a high-profile couple who has several properties. One may later claim that none of the cohab provisions are enforceable because the cohabitation was never exclusive. This is another reason that I prefer to work with a love contract as the document to incorporate all of a couple's lifestyle provisions and legal protections. This way, the agreements within the contract are not lost if someone successfully claims that the cohabitation was not exclusive.

In addition to the typical property distribution provisions, a cohab type of love contract should deal with postbreakup living arrangements. If only one party owns the house or apartment or is the sole tenant on the lease, how much time will the other party have to make alternate arrangements? Will they need financial help to be made whole in this regard? Unmarried couples cannot rely on postbreakup protections in the law. This is why it is essential for both cohabiting partners to protect themselves within a customized legal document.

The following questions should be answered as a starting point for creating the cohab:

- Do either or both parties ever envision getting married to each other? (Any ambivalence in this answer could play into a future claim that there was a promise to marry.)

- Are the parties in similar financial positions? If not, is it agreed that they will contribute to common household expenses in proportion to their respective abilities?
- Is one party relocating or giving up career opportunities for the sake of the relationship? If so, should he or she be made whole in the event of a breakup?
- Will the couple be entertaining clients or business colleagues? If so, it is important to provide that any help to a party's business or career shall not constitute a viable claim to the business or future career earnings.
- Is the house or apartment owned by only one of the parties? If so, it is important to specify that no maintenance or improvements by the nonowner shall result in any rights to the property. If, for example, one party redecorates the home or takes care of the landscaping or other maintenance, he may later try to assert a claim to the property based on his contribution to its value. This is sometimes referred to as a sweat equity claim. It is important to note that most of these claims are unsuccessful. Just because I hang some drapes in my boyfriend's living room does not mean that I can successfully lay claim to part of his house. What we are really trying to prevent, though, is someone from even asserting a claim. Whether or not a flimsy claim will ultimately prevail in court does nothing to relieve me of the agita of dealing with it for months or years before I prevail in court. Often a party asserting a claim is hoping for a settlement or "money to go away." By dealing with the issue in writing on the front end, we can prevent the claim from ever being made.
- Will the nonowner partner be allowed to remain in the home for a certain period of time after the breakup? If so, under what conditions? Will his financial contribution requirement be increased? Will he be allowed to bring (*ahem*) guests over? Will his right to stay be terminated in the event that the breakup was occasioned by his infidelity or other bad behavior episode?
- Will a joint bank account be established for household expenses? If so, we want to include a provision that prevents

ownership claims to the house based on mortgage or property tax payments from the joint account.

- Are there or will there be pet members of the household? If so,
their custody should be decided in advance (see chapter 4).

- If the parties are in unequal financial positions, will the
poorer party need some help to get settled in the event of a
breakup? If so, should this help be forfeited in the event that
the breakup is occasioned by that party's infidelity or other
bad behavior?

Living Together Should Also Cause Us to Deal with a Host of Nonfinancial Issues

Do you want to be able to make healthcare and medical treatment
decisions for each other in the event of a hospitalization? If so, it
is critically important for you to create health-care proxies naming
each other as the health-care agent. Without this document in place,
parents, brothers, and sisters can assert rights to make your health-
care decisions to the exclusion of your partner.

Do you want to give each other access to and control over your
assets and business dealings? If so, then you will want to create powers
of attorney naming each other as financial agents with power to act
in the event of one's physical or mental incapacity. Giving someone
power of attorney can be a difficult decision. It may be a no-brainer
for a firmly established couple. It can be a riskier proposition for a
new relationship. Without a power of attorney in place, however, no
one will be legally able to pay bills or transact other business in the
event of temporary or permanent incapacity. A court would become
involved and probably appoint a person of their choosing to have
oversight and control of your finances. To make matters worse, your
assets would be used to pay this person!

A good solution for many couples is to customize the power of
attorney to prevent the removal of assets. The agent would then be

allowed to transact business, pay bills, and administer affairs but would not be allowed to make gifts to herself or put your real estate into her own name.

If you decide to create health-care proxies and powers of attorney, then your cohabitation agreement should clearly set forth that they are to be revoked in the event of a breakup. The laws of every state automatically provide that divorced parties' rights under these advance directives are terminated. Unmarried partners, however, need to terminate these rights themselves. Otherwise your ex could well be making life-and-death medical decisions for you!

What provisions do you want to make for each other at death? The laws of every state provide surviving spouses with certain automatic property rights. This is not the case with unmarried surviving partners. Estate dispositions to nonspouses can trigger estate tax issues. A competent attorney should be consulted to deal with tax issues as well as potential challenges to the estate plan. As a general rule, you are free to leave your assets to anyone that you choose. However, if it is done through your will, then the plan is subject to challenges from your next of kin. Remember, all wills go to probate. The laws of every state provide that your closest relatives or "heirs at law" be notified when your will is admitted to probate. They would then be free to make a challenge to the will. Without the will, they would receive the assets by virtue of state default or intestate distribution rules. Therefore, many relatives feel they have nothing to lose by asserting a challenge. This is because attorneys often take these cases on what is known as a contingency arrangement. This gives the attorney a portion of any recovery they are able to make. As is the case with so many legal claims, the fact that the claim is without real merit does not mean that it won't cause delays and general misery for everyone involved. As an attorney, I often tell my clients that a given claim is totally without merit. In the next breath, I often recommend that they offer the claimant "a few bucks to go away." The sad reality is that defending against a meritless claim can wind up costing a person much more than settling it.

How can we avoid involving our wacky relatives in the probate process? The answer is to avoid the probate process. This means using a trust instead of a will to distribute assets upon death (see chapter 8).

As with the advance directives, the cohabitation agreement should provide that any estate distributions in each other's favor are to be revoked in the event of a breakup.

Takeaways

1. All people who are living together should create a cohabitation type of love contract (cohab) to deal with distribution of property and custody of pets upon breakup.
2. The cohab should give the nonowner a certain amount of time before he or she must leave the house upon breakup.
3. If you never plan to get married, say so within the cohab.
4. Firmly established couples should create powers of attorney and health-care proxies to allow health-care decisions to be made and financial matters to be handled in the event of incapacity.
5. Cohabiting partners should create a trust rather than a will as their estate distribution plan, in order to prevent relatives from creating delays within the will's probate process.

4

PROTECTING FIDO AND FLUFFY

There are two types of legal structures that are needed to protect our furry family members. First, their care and custody needs to be agreed upon in the event of the pet parents' breakup. Next, each pet parent needs to make arrangements within the context of his or her estate planning documents to ensure that there is as seamless a transition as possible for orphaned pets.

The "Pet-Nup"

This is a clause within any of the love contracts (prenup, postnup, or cohab types) wherein the couple establishes who gets custody of each pet they currently have or may later adopt. Without an agreement in place, a court will likely deal with pets in the same manner as household possessions. This is because the laws of every state consider pets to be the legal equivalent of personal property. Accordingly, whoever can establish proof of purchase will typically be awarded custody. This default rule may not result in the pet being with the person best able to provide care, space, time, and attention.

WYATT AND KATIE'S STORY

When Wyatt and Katie married, Wyatt was a police officer who retired early because of an injury that left him permanently disabled, and Katie was a hedge fund manager who worked eighty hours per week. In an effort to relieve some of Wyatt's boredom, Katie surprised him with two border collies. Over the next three years, Daisy and Romulus became Wyatt's constant companions. He was a regular at the neighborhood dog run and pet-friendly coffee shop. He made several new human friends. Unfortunately for Katie, Wyatt fell in love with one of his fellow pet parents and asked Katie for a divorce. Katie was angry and bitter, because she viewed her intense work hours as an investment in their joint future. She felt that Wyatt was an ingrate who had deceived her. She adopted a scorched-earth policy in their breakup and was determined to take the dogs away from Wyatt in order to cause him maximum suffering. Wyatt's attorney presented the court with reams of vet bills and had witnesses from the neighborhood prepared to testify that they had never once seen Katie walk or otherwise engage with the dogs. The judge, however, was not interested in any evidence other than the copy of the bill of sale that Katie's attorney was able to present to the court.

> The traditional rule can be summed up as "who bought the pet gets the pet." For Daisy and Romulus, application of this archaic rule resulted in them living with Katie. Absolutely no consideration was given to the fact that Katie's work schedule was not conducive to their need for activity and affection. It was, quite simply, a rotten result.

Over the course of the past few years, a handful of enlightened judges have begun contemplating the "best interests" of the pets when deciding a custody dispute. There are also a few state legislators floating the idea of changing the law to require consideration of the pets' best interests when determining custody. Sweeping changes in the law, however, often take many years. In the meantime, it is up to responsible pet parents everywhere to work out custody issues ahead of time. The pet-nup clause within a love contract requires a couple to examine the nature and quality of each pet parent's relationship to existing pets. Several factors that my clients incorporate into their contracts follow:

1. Who provides the pet with more exercise, stimulation, and affection? Who arranges needed medical care and grooming? Who provides for socialization and facilitates pet friendships? Who takes the lead in ensuring that a pet's optimal nutritional needs are met? Here, we look at who feeds the pet unhealthy table scraps, who looks to save a few dollars by buying cheap pet food, and who buys filtered water for the human members of the family yet gives the pets tap water to drink. Who best promotes the pet's self-esteem by speaking in positive and encouraging tones? Who ensures that a pet has proper outerwear and footwear for cold weather outings? (If you think any of this is silly, please relinquish your future custody claims to your partner now.)

2. Who will likely be in a better future position to provide adequate space and financial resources for the pet's optimal quality of life?

3. Could a shared custody arrangement work? Depending upon geographic proximity, this could involve alternating weeks or months.

4. Are there children in the household? If so, I recommend incorporating a presumption that pet custody mirror child custody. The law does not allow for advance contractual child custody agreements. So here, we are simply providing that the pets and children will stay together.

5. Select your own decision maker. No matter how comprehensive and forward thinking our pet clause is, there will still be occasions when the parties vehemently disagree on custody. Given the as yet unenlightened state of our statutory and case law, both parties should resolve to stay out of a courtroom at all costs. As an attorney, I am sometimes asked by the parties to be the agreed-upon default decision maker. Whether you select an attorney, a trusted friend, or a tribunal-type arrangement, it is critically important that you give your arbiter clear tools with which to make an informed custody decision. I provide that a pet psychologist or certified animal behavior specialist interview the pet and evaluate the nature and quality of its interactions with each pet parent. I also allow each pet parent to provide up to five witnesses who can vouch for his or her pet-parenting fitness and ability—or the other party's lack thereof. As a *last* resort, we ask each pet parent to submit to a polygraph and answer questions about whether he or she has ever been unkind or insensitive to this pet or any other pet.

Beyond the threshold custody issue, the couple should consider whether they wish to provide some type of visitation privileges to the other party. This may be appropriate when both partners have strong and long-standing connections to the pet. If an ongoing pet-parenting relationship is envisioned for the noncustodial pet parent, we should also consider the possibility of him or her contributing financially toward the costs of care.

The pet-nup clause can also be used to resolve pet-related disputes within an intact relationship. I often work with couples in "mixed relationships." When a devoted animal lover is sharing a household with a mere animal liker, several issues need to be dealt with. For example, how many pets is too many? This is a frequent bone of contention for the couples I work with. Some seek to establish limits on the number of pets acquired. Many cat parents have two sets of kitties—those who live indoors and rescues who stay outside. Some couples agree that indoor cats not be replaced with outdoor cats when they die.

How much should be spent on the pets? There are probably more fights over this issue than any other pet-related controversy. It isn't just celebrities who indulge their barking babies with spa appointments, organic treats, seasonal wardrobes, and psychologists. When one partner views these expenditures as obscene, then there must be a negotiation. This starts with a compilation of one month's actual expenditures. The pet liker (or pet "tolerator") counters with a figure they view as reasonable. Some couples agree on an average of the two. Other pet lovers agree on the lower figure as a "line item" in the monthly household budget but then make up the shortfall from their separate or discretionary "mad money."

I have one client who gradually emptied her 401K by paying for her pets' veterinary bills. Many kind-hearted people have ended up being wiped out because of pet expenses. Yes, everyone should do with their money as they wish. However, within the context of a committed relationship, shouldn't both parties have information and an opportunity to make compromises in advance of establishing a joint household?

Estate Planning for Families with Pets

We know that pets bestow a wide variety of physical and psychological benefits on their human parents. Studies show that pet parents have lower blood pressure, are less depressed, have reduced feelings of isolation, and live longer than their counterparts living in "human only" households. Homes with dogs are also less likely to be victim-ized by intruders. Why, then, are so many seniors reluctant to wel-come a new pet into their homes? A big reason cited by my clients is the likelihood that the pet will outlive them. They feel it is unfair to adopt a pet and then leave it all alone at death.

Fortunately, with appropriate legal documents in place, it is pos-sible to orchestrate a smooth transition plan for furry loved ones upon the death of their human parents.

First, let's look at what not to do. The most common strategies in estate planning are not the most effective when it comes to dealing with pets. One can't, for example, leave assets to a pet. As discussed earlier, a pet is still legally regarded as one's property. It is, therefore, logically and legally impossible to "leave property to property." A bequest made directly to a pet is considered to be void under the law in every state. Absent a lengthy and complicated reformation proceeding in which a court attempts to craft an equitable solution, the attempted gift to the pet will lapse and go to the default or "resid-uary" beneficiaries under the will. If no alternate beneficiaries are named, then a genealogist may be called in to hunt down the dece-dent's next of kin. It would then be up to these lucky relatives to do the right thing by the pets. Placing trust in people you may never have met is probably not a wise strategy.

Some pet owners choose, instead, to place their trust in friends and relatives that they know well. This arrangement involves naming a human beneficiary under the will. This person is then given verbal instructions as to how the bequest should be used for the care and maintenance of the animals. This type of plan falls under the cate-gory of "hope for the best." The human beneficiary may have the best intentions of honoring their promise, but he or she cannot control life's curveballs.

LEANNA AND TINA'S STORY

Leanna and Tina were sisters who never married and never moved out of their childhood home. They lived happily with their eight cats until Leanna died. Her will left everything to Tina. No other provisions were made in the will because Leanna was 100 percent certain that Tina would continue to take care of the kitties. What Leanna didn't foresee was that Tina would develop dementia and no longer be able to live at home. A distant niece was appointed by the court as Aunt Tina's "conservator" (because Tina failed to name her own agent within a power of attorney—see chapter 13). The niece arranged for the house to be sold. Aunt Tina was placed in a nursing home, and the kitties were handed off to an animal shelter. Because Tina had no legal planning documents in place by the time she developed dementia, she ended up dying without a will. Whatever money hadn't gone to the nursing home by that time went to the niece as Tina's next of kin. The bottom line here is that once assets go to a human being, good intentions alone cannot protect those assets from their own future possible liabilities, including divorce, judgment creditors, and scam artists.

Most states now allow for a more nuanced approach to pet planning in the form of "pet trusts." These can be created and funded during one's life but are most commonly formed by a will or trust and only funded upon death. The arrangement requires that a "pet-care appointee" be named. This is the individual who will be charged with ensuring that the animals are properly cared for. This person may or may not have physical custody of the pets. In addition to designating the appointee, one must also fund the trust with a specific amount of money. This is where the planning can become tricky. A good rule of thumb is to estimate the pet's life expectancy and then multiply the number of remaining years by what you spend on pet food, veterinary bills, and grooming in a given year. This number would be expressed in the will as a formula, because we (thankfully) do not know the year of our death. Adding a 4 percent inflation cushion is also a good idea.

The pet trust must then designate a remainder beneficiary who will receive whatever is left over in the trust upon the death of the pet(s). Most of my clients want the individual who served as the pet care appointee to receive the remaining trust assets. This is understandable and works well in many cases. However, it is important to at least consider the potential for a conflict of interest here.

MILLIE'S STORY

Several years ago, I helped my client Millie establish a pet trust within her will for her five cats. Millie's estate consisted of a duplex apartment on the Upper West Side of Manhattan and a brokerage account worth several million dollars. The entire estate was to go to the pet trust. This provided that the cats would continue to live in the apartment and all household expenses would continue to be paid from the brokerage account by Millie's friend, Ralph, who was named the appointee. The trust provided that upon the death of the last cat, Ralph was to receive the Manhattan apartment and other assets remaining in the trust. Within two years of Millie's death, all five of the cats had died. The statistical likelihood of all five deaths being of natural causes is, in my opinion, pretty remote. The bottom line is that there is definitely the potential for a conflict of interest when the caregiver receives a windfall payment upon the death of his or her charge.

Another approach is to set up the pet trust so that the pet care appointee is paid annually. This payment should cover the pet's expenses and will also factor in a gift to the pet care appointee. Gifts to the appointee are not taxable as income, the way that a salary would be. Upon the death of the pet(s), all remaining trust monies would be paid to a third party, such as an animal rights organization. If you choose the annual payment scenario, you may wish to consider specifically identifying the animals that are to be covered by your trust. This would reduce the possibility of the pet care appointee surreptitiously replacing your pet with another upon its death in order to keep the payments coming.

When I work with pet parents in setting up these trusts, I recommend involving a not-for-profit group in the planning process. Some animal rights organizations are willing to be named as pet care appointee. As mentioned earlier, the appointee does not necessarily have physical custody of the pet but is responsible for arranging an appropriate care plan. There are often informal networks of compassionate animal lovers out there who have limited resources. Uniting them with your furry loved one (who has resources, thanks to your pet trust) can be a win-win—akin to a foster-parenting situation. The not-for-profit appointee will serve as a monitor and ensure that vet visits are up to date and that pet funds are being properly used. Upon the death of your pet, the not-for-profit would receive what is left in the trust.

Planning for our furry loved ones, as with any estate planning, merits a thoughtful and customized approach. It is also a good idea to review your planning with your attorney every few years, as your life and the law will undoubtedly evolve.

Takeaways:

1. Couples with pets should establish custody ahead of time within a love contract. This should be revised periodically to account for changed circumstances.
2. Pet parents should make provisions within their estate planning to minimize disruption to pets upon a pet parent's death.
3. Disagreements over the number of pets in the household and/or the amount of spending on them can be hammered out within a love contract.

5

STALE DOCUMENTS CAN COST YOU

U pon completion of their legal planning documents, clients sometimes express their relief that it's "done." My response is that one's estate planning is never done. Gone are the days when you did a simple will with your lawyer and then wished each other a good life and parted company.

I recommend that all love contracts and other legal planning be reviewed at least once a year. This will enable the parties to measure progress to date, identify areas where more work is needed, and possibly add some new lifestyle provisions.

Legal planning should be viewed as a process rather than an event. Life changes, laws change, and your relationships with your beneficiaries change, as does their ability to manage money. A good estate and asset protection plan will enable you to amend the documents to make sure they are responsive to life as it exists at any given point in time.

LENNY AND ANNA'S STORY

Lenny and Anna did their wills in 1988. In the wills, they left everything to each other, and then upon the death of the second spouse, all of the assets were to go equally to their three children, Susie, Johnny, and Danny. Then, in 1998, they got some bad advice from their trusted friend. Roger worked as a paralegal in a big law firm. He offered to help Lenny and Anna transfer their home into their kids' names. Roger's mother went into a nursing home several years earlier, and his family lost the house to pay the exorbitant monthly bills. He wanted to save Lenny and Anna from such a fate. He had seen the lawyers in his office do deed transfers hundreds of times and would be able to do it for his friends for free. Lenny, however, had serious qualms about giving up ownership of his home. He remembered hearing a horror story about someone putting his house into his son's name. The son then went through a messy divorce, and part of the value of the house was awarded to the son's ex-wife. He appreciated Roger's good intentions but decided to consult a lawyer to carefully assess his legal options.

The attorney applauded Lenny's instincts in not "turning over" ownership of the house to the kids. If he had done so, the attorney advised, Lenny would have lost all of his annual property tax exemptions. Also, the kids would have taken the house with a built-in capital gains problem. This is because a gifted asset goes to the new owner with a "cost basis" equal to the original purchase price. Even if the kids did let Anna and Lenny live out their lives in the house, they would be hit with a huge capital gains penalty upon selling the house after the death of the second parent. In other words, with the simple transfer of ownership, the kids would be taxed on the difference between the parents' original purchase price (forty years ago) and the ultimate sale price at death. Instead, the attorney suggested that Lenny and Anna create a "life estate." In effect, the children's names would be on the deed now, but the parents would retain legal owner-ship rights during their lives. The analogy the attor-ney used was a CD at the bank. The parents would be the current owners, and the kids would be the beneficiaries upon their death. This sounded reasonable, so Lenny and Anna transferred the home to the three children "sub-ject to Lenny and Anna's lifetime ownership rights."

Some years after the life estate was created, life threw a curveball. Their daughter, Susie, died while zip-lining in Costa Rica with her new husband, Raoul. After the memorial service, Lenny and Anna went back to the attorney to have Susie's name taken off of the deed. They were baffled and horrified to learn that they had permanently given that one-third future own-ership interest away. Susie's one-third interest would pass according to the terms of her will, because it was legally hers at the time of death. The problem was that Susie was only twenty-seven and didn't have a will yet. When someone doesn't have a will, his or her state of residence has one as a default. And so it was that New York's "intestate" laws provided that Raoul, whom Lenny and Anna hadn't even met yet, owned one-third of the future interest in their home.

The takeaway from Lenny and Anna's horrible but true story is that we should always retain a set of "handcuff keys" when doing legal planning. In the case of the life estate, Anna and Lenny could have easily retained something called a "special power of appointment." The deed should have transferred the home to the three children subject not only to Anna and Lenny's lifetime ownership rights but also to Anna and Lenny's power to reassign the children's interests between and among their lineal descendants (e.g., children and grandchildren).

This retained right helps parents react not only to a tragedy but also to other changed circumstances. What if Susie hadn't died and had become the primary caregiver to her parents as they advanced in years? What if Johnny and Danny had great intentions but were always so busy with their families that they only saw their parents a few times a year? Is it fair that Johnny and Danny receive the same share as Susie, who visits her parents daily, takes them shopping, and takes them to doctor's appointments? As I tell my clients, it isn't my job to decide what is "fair" and what isn't (except in my own will . . .). Instead, my job is to make sure that my clients are legally able to change their minds within the context of changed circumstances.

I have seen countless curveballs in my twenty years as an estate planning attorney. I have seen so much that I have given up trying to anticipate every possible contingency when initially preparing documents. Instead, I make sure that there are controls put in place, so my clients are never in a miserable situation that they are stuck with.

The list of factors that should cause us to reevaluate our legal planning seems to me to be endless. Let's revisit Lenny and Anna's standard wills, which left everything to the survivor and then later to the children. What if the children are all fine and they are equally loving and helpful to their parents? Should Lenny and Anna still ever consider revisiting that will? It should definitely be revisited and changed in the event that either one of them develops dementia or some other long-term condition. If either one of them is no longer physically or cognitively capable of handling finances, it could be a great mistake for him or her to inherit everything. Instead, the well spouse may choose to create a trust for the lifetime benefit of the other. If Lenny were sick or otherwise incapacitated, then Anna's will would thus be amended to provide that all assets be given to the named trustee(s) to be held, managed, and administered for the lifetime benefit of Lenny. All assets would be available for his needs and wants. However, because they are not actually owned by him, they would be protected, to the greatest extent possible, against his health-care liabilities as well as con artists and future possible love interests.

Changes may also be warranted if one or more of the children has a problem such as substance abuse, gambling, multiple failed marriages, or compulsive spending. It would probably be a big mistake to allow an outdated will to leave his or her assets in his or her own name. A trust would be a far better option to hold the inheritance of any beneficiary with temporary or permanent money management woes (see chapter 8).

Revisiting one's planning is also a wise idea if a child moves back home. Was the move back because she needed help or because her help was needed to care for an ailing parent? In either case, thought must be given to altering the initially equal distribution under the will. If an unequal distribution is contemplated—whether or not it's because a beneficiary needs or deserves the extra help—it is a very good idea to prepare the others for this. Failure to do so can tear the family apart later.

THE FARRELL FAMILY'S STORY

Consider the Farrell family, who ended up at war because of an outdated estate plan. John Farrell updated his will in 1993 after the death of his wife. The new will left everything in equal shares to his three children, Mary, Gina, and Thomas. Following his stroke in 2006, Gina came home to care for him "temporarily" while she looked for a new job. Several years into this arrangement, John promised Gina that he would update his will to provide that she get the house upon his death.

Neither the trip to the lawyer nor the new job came to
pass prior to John's death in 2013.

After the funeral, Mary and Thomas graciously
informed Gina that they had no objection to her staying in the house for a few weeks while she made alternate living arrangements. In the meantime, they wanted
to put the house on the market right away so that the
sale proceeds could be split three ways pursuant to
the will. Gina was flabbergasted that they were not
going to voluntarily honor Dad's verbal wish that she
keep the house and continue to live there.

Gina promptly changed the locks, bunkered down,
and refused to let the real estate broker in. Mary and
Thomas hired an eviction lawyer as well as a probate
lawyer to enforce the three-way split called for under
the 1993 will. Gina then hired a lawyer to contest
the will and try to enforce her father's verbal promise regarding the house. As tensions and anger levels increased, in-laws became involved. Thomas's wife
came up with the idea that they also sue Gina for the
fair market value of back rent that she didn't pay her
father from 2006 through 2013. Gina countered that she
should be paid the fair market value of the home-care
services that she provided her father during that same
period. She argued that by caring for their father at
home, he avoided a costly nursing home stay that would
have likely consumed the value of the entire estate.

The case ended up settling. The claims for back
rent and care services rendered were both dropped.
Mary and Thomas each agreed to accept 25 percent of
the fair market value of the home. Gina has ten years
to pay them off. Her hope is that she will find a new
job and be able to do this without having to sell
the home. Prospects for her job search, though, are
questionable. Seven years caring for an ailing parent

aren't exactly a plus on her tech field résumé. Needless to say, relations between the kids are permanently damaged.

Periodic estate planning review sessions should be a time for
you to confide in your attorney. Why bother having an attorney if
you don't totally confide in them? I feel that it is essential for my
clients to tell me everything. I need to know about their health
concerns, the states of their marriages, concerns about children
who have developed substance-abuse issues, and gambling problems, as well as other special needs. Does your new daughter-in-law
spend money like a drunken sailor? Your estate planning attorney
needs to know. Haven't spoken to your brother and his wife since
Thanksgiving 1992? Your attorney needs to know. Why are these
very personal matters relevant to your estate planning? Because you
are more likely to be involved in a legal dispute with a family member or love interest than with a stranger. This can be a fiercely con-
tested divorce battle or a bitter fight with siblings over a parent's
will. Good estate planning is designed to keep you from a courtroom battle with someone you once broke bread and/or shared a
pillow with.

Not telling your lawyer about every aspect of your life (*ahem*—
special relationships) can result in full frontal estate warfare later.

CHARLES'S STORY

Remember Charles Kuralt? He spent many years traveling across the country to bring us interesting stories. The people, places, and events that he reported
on seem boring when compared to the story he left us
after his death. It turned out that the married news-
man had a decades-long relationship with a woman named
Patricia Shannon.

Several months before his death, Kuralt transferred twenty acres of property in Montana to Ms. Shannon. In a misguided attempt to keep things simple, he disguised the gift as a sale. Instead of simply making a gift of the real estate, Kuralt made a gift to Shannon of $80,000 (without filing the required gift tax returns). She then used this money to "purchase" the twenty acres from Kuralt. This left him with ninety remaining acres.

In June of 1997, Charles Kuralt was hospitalized for a mysterious health issue. In a now-famous letter he wrote from his hospital bed, he sought to assure Pat Shannon that he would pursue legal steps so that she would inherit the remaining Montana property:

June 18, 1997. Dear Pat-Something is terribly wrong with me and they can't figure out what. After cat-scans and a variety of cardiograms, they agree it's not lung cancer or heart trouble or a blood clot. I seem to be getting worse, barely able to get out of bed, but still have high hopes for recovery . . . if only I can get a diagnosis! Curiouser and curiouser! I'll keep you informed. I'll have the lawyer visit the hospital to be sure you inherit the rest of the place in MT if it comes to that. I send love to you. Hope things are better there! Love, C.

Kuralt died on July 4, 1997. He never did get around to having a lawyer change his will. That didn't stop Shannon from laying claim to the additional ninety acres in a Montana court. Meanwhile, back in New York, Kuralt's widow and daughters from a prior marriage filed his 1994 will for probate in New York County Surrogate's Court. The will left everything to them.

What do you think Ms. Shannon's chances would be, given that Kuralt didn't get around to making the new will to give her the property? Ten out of ten trust and estate attorneys would predict that that she had no chance. The document that she filed in Surrogate's Court was not a will but, rather, the letter in which Kuralt expressed his intention to change his will. Kuralt's family objected vehemently. In a surprise decision, the Montana court sided with Shannon.

The next surprise is who paid the estate taxes due on the Montana property. Any guesses? Kuralt's New York family! This is because his simple will from 1994 contained the boilerplate "tax apportionment" clause contained in 99 percent of wills: "I direct that all estate or inheritance taxes on all property passing at my death, whether through this will or otherwise, be paid as an expense of administration of my probate (passing under this will) estate." This meant that Kuralt's girlfriend received the property free and clear, and Kuralt's wife and kids had to pay an extra $350,000 in estate taxes!

This entire fiasco could have been avoided if Kuralt had confided in his attorney about his extra-marital relationship.

Not all life changes will require one's will to be updated. Just because a will is old does not mean that it must necessarily be redone. If a will was validly executed fifteen years ago, it remains valid today. If my daughter marries and has a new last name, this does not warrant a new will. If a beneficiary predeceases me, I should not have to redo my will provided that I built in an appropriate "default taker" when I originally created the will.

If there is a change that you wish to make, then it is a good idea to redo the will in its entirety. Some people prefer to utilize a "codicil" if the change to be made is a relatively small one. A codicil can be thought of as an abbreviated form of a will that sets forth only the changed item. This document does not replace the original will but is used in conjunction with it. I strongly advise my clients against using a codicil to make changes. To the extent that both the original will and the codicil must both be subjected to the probate process, the proceeding will almost certainly take longer. The witnesses to the codicil will likely be different from the witnesses to the original will. This will necessitate testimony from four separate witnesses or an examination of four affidavits that were sworn to at the time the will was executed. The codicil may have made sense back in the days before computers, when wills were typed out and could not be saved electronically. Then, an attorney would have certainly charged a client less for a two-to-three-page codicil than for a new fifteen-page will. Today, however, the wills are stored electronically, and a change can be made very easily.

The situation that prompts the biggest number of will-change requests is a falling out or changed relationship with a named beneficiary. We are legally able to totally disinherit anyone with the exception of a surviving spouse. Absent a pre- or postnuptial agreement, a surviving spouse is entitled to one-third of the estate. Louisiana, which still follows certain provisions of the Napoleonic Code, is the only state that requires anything be left to surviving children. In the other forty-nine states, we are able to get mad at our children and disinherit them at will.

Reasons for disinheriting or reducing a child's estate interest vary. Holiday arguments are a leading cause. I experience an uptick in change requests in the week after a big holiday. I try to schedule these appointments as far out as my clients will allow me. This often gives the family members a chance to cool off and work things out on their own. If they remain adamant about disinheriting a child, it is important to do it correctly so that the family will not be subjected to full frontal will warfare later.

When unequal distributions to beneficiaries are contemplated, or when one has an idea that there will be other reasons for a protracted estate administration process, it is a good idea to consider an *in terrorem* clause. The upshot of this clause is that whoever challenges the will loses everything that he or she otherwise would have received thereunder. This is a typical *in terrorem* clause:

> If any named beneficiary shall institute a challenge or objection to this, my Last Will and Testament, then any bequest in his her or their favor shall be forfeited, and distributed as if the objectant had predeceased me, with no issue surviving me.

The key to successfully employing an *in terrorem* clause is to leave the would-be objectant with a big enough stake that they don't want to gamble. It is a huge mistake to leave a child a token $1 bequest and then think that the *in terrorem* clause will suffice to prevent him from instigating a will contest. The $1 bequest has the exact opposite effect and will almost guarantee a contest. This is because the person has nothing to lose.

Avoiding a will contest is a little like playing chess in that we need to anticipate what a likely challenger's legal claims will be. The most common challenges to a will center around fraud, duress, and undue influence.

The basis of a fraud challenge is that the testator (person making the will) didn't realize the document he was signing was a will. A contestant might allege that Mom thought she was signing a contract for a new wireless carrier rather than a will leaving everything to one child.

The bases for duress and undue influence claims overlap somewhat. The gist of each is that the testator was not operating independently and the resulting document reflects the input of outsiders. If you want to prevent challengers from making these claims, it helps to imagine what their arguments will be. If I represent a child who was cut out of a will, and the will leaves everything to another child, here is how I go about attacking it in court. My first question for the attorney draftsman is always: "Who else was present in the office at the time the will was made?" Was the testator alone, or was she accompanied by the child who inherits everything? I am thrilled when I hear that the child who gets everything under the will was in the room at all times. This really helps me make an argument that the parent was not acting freely and could have been subjected to coaching or pressure by that child. I then want to know how the attorney was selected. I love it when I hear that the attorney previously did work for the child who is getting everything. Was the parent living independently? Or was the parent living with the child who inherited everything? Living arrangements can cut both ways. When representing a challenger, I will argue that the testator was not acting independently when she was relying upon one child for all of life's necessities. She may not have felt able to say no to the child's request that the will be redone to leave everything to him. On the other hand, when I represent the child with whom the parent lived, I will argue that it is perfectly reasonable for a parent to leave everything to the child who cared enough to take her in and help her with everything. We should always anticipate a contest when there is an unequal distribution. One way to guard against this is to ensure that the attorney meets alone with the testator. Whenever I have an adult child accompany a parent into my conference room, I promptly escort them back to the waiting room. This gives me the opportunity to ask questions of my client designed to elicit whether she truly wishes to favor one child in the will. When I am certain that this is what my client truly wants, then I make very clear file notes to this effect, and I will also document that she was alone with me. This way, if I am not around anymore at the time of the will contest, my file notes will help the will survive an attack.

After doing everything possible to draft and execute the will in such a way that it will survive a probate challenge, I urge my clients to create a trust so that probate can be avoided in its entirety. Again, we should all have a will. However, the goal is not to have to use it. See chapter 8 to determine which type of trust may make sense for your situation.

Takeaways

1. Force yourself to muddle through the boring language in your documents.

2. Question your attorney until you are satisfied that you understand how the language pertains to your unique situation.

3. It is extremely important that you confide in your attorney. There isn't much that he or she hasn't heard before. They are legally bound to keep your secrets.

4. Keep in regular contact with your lawyer. He or she will let you know when and if documents need to be updated.

5. Also, don't assume that verbal promises between and among family members will be upheld. Recollections vary, expectations differ, and in-laws can complicate matters. Remember, if it is important, put it in writing!

6. Special situations require special estate planning. A simple will does not adequately protect your loved ones if you are married and also have a nonmarital relationship. This is true whether a lawyer drafts the will or if it is a fill-in-the-blanks "bargain."

7. To avoid a will war at your death, avoid having to probate the will. Implementing a trust rather than a will can help your family avoid the three-ring circus of probate that can play out publicly over the course of many months. A properly drafted and funded trust can ensure that property passes to your loved ones automatically and privately without the need for court involvement.

6

CHILDREN AND MONEY

The central premise of all estate planning is how best to structure an inheritance so that the next generation has maximum financial security. We seek to protect our children from an array of outside forces capable of separating them from their money. A good estate plan will also protect a child from his or her own poor money decisions and financial mismanagement. Before delving into the legal structures we can use to accomplish these goals, I encourage all parents to help their children develop strong internal financial foundations. Ensuring that our children have solid and responsible money habits will supercharge the efficacy of the legal structures we create.

Today's children have more of just about everything compared to what their parents and grandparents had growing up. It is not unusual to see a twelve-year-old with his or her own TV, computer, and cell phone. They have all manner of gadgets, gizmos, and toys. They have everything except, perhaps, the security and self-discipline that only comes from having mastered the art of delayed gratification. Being awash in all of this easily acquired "stuff" leaves today's youngsters at a distinct disadvantage as they enter adulthood. I've never once heard any of my children's friends talk about "saving up" for something. Rather, I hear, "I'm going to tell my mom that I want X, Y, or Z." This is not setting the stage for a lifetime of financial security based on a healthy relationship with money.

One hundred years ago, the personal savings rate was in excess of ten percent. Though many of our immigrant ancestors were barely scraping by, they clearly had better savings habits and skills than many of us do. They knew how to stretch their pennies and viewed being thrifty as a virtue. They were also totally free from the tremendous pressures exerted by modern-day advertising and consumer credit industries.

Prior to television and the nonstop barrage of commercials, our grandparents bought something only when three stars were in alignment: they needed it, they wanted it, and *they had money to buy it*. We modern consumers have been convinced that we need and want an endless array of stuff. Billions of dollars and very brilliant minds have been deployed with the sole objective of altering our perception of what it means to need something. Lost along the way was the minor detail about having the cash on hand to buy these things.

The seductive and plentiful supply of easy credit heads our way by late adolescence. The credit comes to us years before brain maturation is complete. Scientists tell us that right-brain functioning, which is what controls our ability to delay gratification and make responsible choices, is not even fully developed until our midtwenties.

Any present or former college student knows how hard credit card companies market to students. This is an unfair fight on several levels. The students are really still adolescents. It is fairly easy for credit card companies to seduce them with the instant power to have and do anything they want. It will take many painful years, though, for our nation's young people to realize that the beckoning pieces of plastic actually sapped them of freedom and power.

Those who took the bait and lived a brief credit-fueled high life can expect to be in repayment for many years. The average American carries a credit card balance of approximately $8,000. If he or she is making minimum payments on this amount, with an interest rate of 18 percent, it will take more than twenty-six years to be out of debt! The total amount repaid to the credit card company at the end of the 26.6 years will be $19,423!

Once the credit binge is over, the "victim" joins the sorry ranks of American debtors. Debt truly is a heavy burden for anyone to bear and is responsible for a whole host of problems for individuals and families.

Consider the number of people who have second and even third jobs to make ends meet. They now have less leisure time, exercise, and rest and thereby cause the entire family to suffer stress.

The picture for the credit card companies is much rosier. Having successfully lobbied Congress to restrict the availability of bankruptcy protections for consumers, the "creditor predators" are reaping the rewards. The average American now works four hours each week, simply to make interest payments. This would seem to prove the point of the biblical scripture "The borrower is servant to the lender" (Prov. 22:7).

Some young people who are pinned under a debt avalanche will turn to their parents to bail them out. This may seem like a good strategy on paper. The reasoning is that the credit card company shouldn't be getting a windfall in the form of high interest payments. Instead, the theory goes that the parents pay off the debt and then the child makes monthly payments to the parents. In reality, this can cause tremendous intrafamily difficulties. I have seen clients do this, against my advice, and thereby jeopardize their own retirement planning. Children begin making regular repayments to their parents, but then something unavoidable (always) comes up. Any amounts forgiven by the parent can end up causing resentment on the part of the other children.

There are, in my opinion, only two things that we, as parents, can do to prevent children from falling victim to the creditor predators:

1. Kids need to hear the word *no*! I know all too well that it can be easier to say yes—whether it is candy at the supermarket

checkout, the latest video game, a new handheld device, or a smartphone. I believe that kids crave boundaries. By giving them what they want when they want it, we are depriving them of the virtuous joy that only comes from diligently planning and saving toward one's goal. By regularly forcing children to wait for what they want, we are helping them to hone their delayed gratification capabilities. Remember the classic marshmallow experiment from the 1960s? Children were left alone in a room with a marshmallow. They could either eat it or wait for the adult to return to the room and have two marshmallows. Follow-up studies proved that the children who were able to hold out were more successful in every measurable category later in life. Saying no is indeed one of the most important things that we as parents can do.

2. We need to set the example. We can't tell our kids that they must live within their means if they see us with too many cars in the driveway and flat-screen TVs in the house. The financial boot camp exercise (see chapter 10) is an effective tool with which to make saving money a shared family goal.

Legal Structures to Protect Children

Protecting our smallest loved ones requires more than heartfelt intentions. Without carefully constructed legal provisions, a judge and his golf buddies can very well end up in charge of the children's future.

ALAN'S STORY

Consider the case of Alan Kurtz. He was, by all outward appearances, a very successful dentist who lived in a large new home with his attractive wife and three young daughters. The real story was quite different. Alan was actually deeply in debt and very depressed. For two years, he had been paying only the minimum on his credit cards. He thought that his dental practice would grow if he joined a fancy country club, but the monthly bills were choking him. Eventually, the financial pressures were so severe that he stopped opening all of the monthly bills. He contemplated suicide on more than one occasion. He finally decided that he couldn't stand it anymore. He made plans to asphyxiate himself. And so it was on one Sunday morning in the predawn hours, Alan closed the garage door, locked the car doors, and turned on the engine. His efforts succeeded. The greater tragedy, though, was the fact that he took his wife and two of his three daughters with him. This was because the garage was attached to the house. The deadly carbon monoxide seeped into the house over the course of several hours.

Four-year-old Ava was the only survivor. Alan had a will that he and his wife, Holly, executed right after they got married. The wills provided that everything be left to each other, and the remainder would go to any children they had. Was this enough legal protection for little Ava? Not by a long shot. Even though the will was properly done, it failed miserably in two respects. It didn't name a guardian to raise minor children, and it failed to provide that any money intended for the minor be held in trust for her benefit.

The failure to name a guardian for Ava resulted in both sets of grandparents in court for eighteen months fighting over who was best suited to raise the little girl.

No one wants to spend much time thinking about a tragedy that would require someone other than you to raise your kids. Reluctance to deal with this issue causes countless people to put off making or updating their wills. I recall spending more than a little bit of time mentally replaying Debra Winger's good-bye scene to her kids in *Terms of Endearment*, as I struggled with naming the perfect guardian in my will. Of course, there is no perfect guardian. As it stands, I am still not 100 percent comfortable with the guardian selection I made. I believe, though, that it is better to have a "B+" candidate named than to leave it up to a self-important judge overseeing a squabble among my wacky relatives.

Dr. Kurtz's will also failed because it didn't have a "minor's trust." This meant that in addition to selecting Ava's guardian, the court was responsible for overseeing the child's money. A minor (someone under eighteen or twenty-one depending on your state of residence) is incapable of inheriting money or property directly. Where there is no will or when the will fails to create a "minor's trust," the court typically appoints attorneys to oversee the minor's money as either a "guardian ad litem" or a trustee. As you can imagine, these are paying gigs. Who pays? Little Ava does.

Michael Jackon's estate plan was far superior to that of Dr. Kurtz. First, he named a guardian to have physical custody of his three minor children. His mother, Katharine Jackson, was named primary guardian, and the singer's lifelong friend Diana Ross was named as the back-up guardian of Paris, Prince, and Michael.

Even more impressive was the way Michael Jackson structured his children's inheritances. He went beyond simply holding the money in trust until they reached a stated age. Instead, he provided that each child's share would be held by the trustees (his lawyer and accountant) and given to the children in a staggered fashion. They will each receive one-third at age twenty-five, one-half of the remaining balance at age thirty, and the final distribution at age thirty-five. Prior to the stated ages, the trustees have full discretion to make distributions to and for the benefit of the children. This way, the kids can have their cake and eat it too. They can benefit from the money without it being owned by them outright. This is the best way to protect youngsters from losing property to lawsuits. I guess the King of Pop learned a thing or two about this subject the hard way and didn't want his kids to be such attractive lawsuit defendants.

Whitney Houston's estate plan, on the other hand, resulted in an estimated $2 million dollar payout to Bobbi Kristina Brown upon her twenty-first birthday. This windfall could not possibly have helped poor Bobbi Kristina, as she was dealing with serious life problems.

Helping Children and Grandchildren

It is a very rare situation for all of one's children to be equally financially situated. Most parents have at least one child who constantly needs money. How much should you give her now, and how should you provide for her in your estate later? Consider the following factors.

When a child asks for money, it can be very hard to say no. Here, you should be guided by what you can comfortably give as well as by what you can comfortably afford never to see back again. Your child may have the very best intentions of returning the money to you after the current crisis has passed. By now, I hope you have gotten the message that what is legally in your child's name has become her property. If she gets into a car accident, gets divorced, has judgment creditors, etc., your former money or other asset will be gone.

With this in mind, I advise clients to avoid making very large "vested" (unchangeable) gifts to their children. I see many people who gift money and other property in order to reduce their gross taxable estates or to protect the money against long-term care expenses. (We will discuss better ways of achieving these goals in later chapters.) Yes, the prenuptial agreement can and should clearly state that gifts are to remain separate property. However, it is usually still better to avoid making these gifts in the first place. Remember that an outright gift to children is not only vulnerable in the case of their possible divorces, but it will also be counted against grandchildren applying for college financial aid. The gift will also be in jeopardy if your child runs into any other legal liabilities (think car accident, failed business, etc.). Last, if you should unexpectedly need the money back, and even if your child is willing and able to return it, there may be gift tax consequences to him for doing so, if the amount is greater than $14,000.

For seniors of limited means who may need to qualify for Medicaid, this gift to a child can also cause a penalty if made within five years of a nursing home stay. Gifts to children are not exempted from the five-year penalty calculation. Remember that the annual exclusion of $14,000 exempts gifts only from gift taxes. For more information about the Medicaid program, go to www.myelderlawattorney.com.

If your child is in need of cash for some purpose that you deem worthy, such as a down payment on a house, consider helping him by way of a loan. If it is a bona fide loan, supported by an actual promissory note, then the cash will not be legally treated as the child's property. The money would, therefore, be protected from any of the child's legal liabilities. The parent would then be free to assign or gift the note into a properly drafted trust in order to remove that amount from the gross taxable estate, thereby achieving an important estate planning goal without the downside of an outright gift. A loan, as opposed to a gift, can also obviate a Medicaid penalty to a parent or grandparent.

If you do make any kind of loan to a child, you should create an actual promissory note. A verbal loan or merely noting "loan" on the check will not do the job. There are sample promissory notes on my website. Beyond this, *please consider how you wish the loan to be dealt with upon your death.* Should it be forgiven? Should it be repaid to the estate? A related decision should also be made for significant gifts. Do you wish for the gift to be treated as an advance against your child's share of the estate? Was the gift meant to be in addition to the purportedly equal distribution called for in the will or trust? Your children will surely have different opinions on this. These questions routinely create fodder for years in court if not clearly dealt with ahead of time.

Saying No to Loved Ones

If you are not in a position to comfortably make a gift or a loan to a child, be prepared for her to ask you to cosign her loan from someone else. This could be a mortgage, a personal loan, or a grandchild's student loan. Please consider this long and hard and then say no! Blame it on your financial advisor, your accountant, or me!

People often mistakenly believe that cosigning a loan is no different from providing a reference or recommendation for someone. It sounds pretty harmless. But nothing could be further from the truth. The moment you become a cosigner, the entire value of the new loan appears on your credit report as your obligation. This will affect your debt-to-credit ratio, which will immediately pull down your credit score. Please remember that this does not happen only upon the default of the primary borrower. A lower credit score can make it harder for you to buy or lease your next car and can also allow your credit card companies to spontaneously lower your credit limits and increase your interest rate.

The hardest cosigning request to turn down will come from your beautiful and precious grandchild applying for student loans. In terms of reducing your future financial security, however, college loans can be the worst offenders. As a nation, the combined outstanding student loans hover at $1 trillion. The default rate is at an all-time high. Families cannot rely on the outdated notion that all college debt is necessarily "good debt." Consider the simple facts: the current number of unemployed college graduates exceeds the number of jobs that require a college education. How will an unemployed or underemployed college graduate repay these loans? What about the record numbers of students who don't graduate? These loans don't disappear.

Default rates are greatest for students enrolled in proprietary (for-profit) schools. These schools often have abysmal graduation rates. Unfortunately, they don't have much of an incentive to try to truly help their students graduate. This is because they get the student loan payments whether their students graduate or not. The students, on the other hand, often find it impossible to gain employment that is adequate enough to enable them to repay the loans.

SARAH AND BECKY'S STORY

My client Sarah asked for advice when her granddaughter, Becky, needed a cosigner on her student loan.

Becky had already borrowed the maximum available through federally subsidized loan programs and was now in the private student loan market. Private loans almost always require a cosigner. I literally begged Sarah to say no. I explained that in the event of a default by Becky, Sarah's mortgage-free house could be subject to a lien. Sarah was just getting by on her social security and pension. Where on earth was she going to come up with money to pay off a loan if Becky defaulted? Job prospects for octogenarians are not the greatest. Sarah listened to and understood every word that came out of my mouth. She then proceeded to ignore all of them. Sarah couldn't say no to her beautiful Becky. She assured me that they had a long discussion, and Becky promised that if school didn't work out, for any reason, she would get a job to pay off the student loan. Unfortunately for both of them, Becky was killed in a car accident during her first month of school. Sarah was shocked and disgusted that this horrific twist of fate did nothing to relieve her of the student loan repayment obligation.

If your grandchildren are willing to listen to anything you have to say after your initial *no*, you might suggest the following: in high school, advanced placement courses can garner college-level credits. Beyond this, college-level examination placement tests can rack up more credits for a subject that the student can master by reading commercially available booklets geared to the tests. If a youngster can pick up enough extra credits to complete a degree in three years rather than four years, that is a 25 percent savings on the cost of his college education. Perhaps you are in a position to offer your grandchild a place to live while he attends a college in your area. Your grandchildren should know that you want nothing more than to see them succeed. Offer your creativity and expertise in coming up with solutions to finance college. However, please remember that you are not doing them any favors by jeopardizing your future financial security in the process.

Helping Children after Our Death

In addition to promoting our children's financial security, a good estate plan strives to protect feelings and reduce the chance of conflict between beneficiaries. One of the biggest sources of conflict is perceived inequality in the estate plan.

If it is your intention to provide for an unequal distribution of your estate, careful and thoughtful planning is called for. Inequality can breed resentment and can permanently damage children's relationships with one another. Even if my son is wildly successful and doesn't need a dime of my modest estate, his feelings may still be hurt to see that "Catherine got more."

To reduce feelings of resentment, consider leaving the extra distribution in the form of a separate trust that has one child as the named beneficiary. This will remove these assets from what will pass "equally" to the children through other estate vehicles. For example, if my estate is worth $1 million and I want one child to receive $600,000 and the other child to receive $400,000, I can create a trust during my life to hold $200,000. One child is the named beneficiary. She will receive this automatically upon my death. She and her sister will then split the remaining $800,000 equally by virtue of my will or other trust that names them as equal beneficiaries.

If the unequal distribution is contemplated based on the greater needs of a given beneficiary, you may wish to consider protecting his, her, or their shares in a continuing trust. If, for example, my daughter is very responsible in every way but is simply in a low-paying career, then she will probably not need for her inheritance to be "protected." On the other hand, if the reason my child constantly needs money is because of a gambling problem, out-of-control spending, a substance-abuse issue, serial divorces, or some other impediment that shows no sign of ending, then we should consider a protective trust. The same is true for a child or grandchild with a developmental disability or a long-term illness, or one who is receiving means-tested government program benefits.

The "old school" way of dealing with these issues was to simply omit naming the child with complications in the estate plan. The thought was that the remaining children would "do the right thing." When I am asked to do this by clients who "wish to keep things simple," I tell them about my client Miriam.

MIRIAM'S STORY

Miriam had a severely disabled son living in a group home. She asked me to leave him entirely out of the estate plan and, instead, leave everything to her other two children, Candace and Rose. Miriam's concern was that Todd's eligibility for certain government benefits would be jeopardized if he received a windfall inheritance. I suggested that we create a special trust for Todd's share of the estate. This "special needs trust" is designed to allow a disabled individual to receive benefits from an estate without jeopardizing eligibility for government programs such as Medicaid and SSI. Miriam thought this approach was way too complicated. She was absolutely certain that "her girls" would do the right thing by Todd. Within three years of Miriam's death, however, Rose lost nearly all of her assets, including the money she was holding in a "gentleman's agreement" for Todd, in a Bernie Madoff-type Ponzi scheme. Candace didn't lose her one-half of her mother's estate and is doing her best to make sure that her brother Todd is well taken care of. Candace is a bit resentful of Rose, because she feels that the entire burden of looking after Todd has now fallen upon her.

I pointed out to Candace that she is every bit as capable of losing the remaining one-half of Todd's

assets in the event that she experiences a costly
breakup, develops a dementia-related illness, or dies.
Determined not to allow history to repeat itself, Candace established a special needs trust with what was
left of her one-half of the money earmarked for Todd
from her mother's estate. She named herself as the
trustee of the trust, which allows her to use assets
to supplement (as opposed to supplant or replace)
benefits that Todd receives through state programs.
Candace can, for example, use trust assets to pay
for vacations, clothing, and entertainment for Todd.
When I asked Candace to give me the name of a backup
or alternate trustee who could act in the event, she
couldn't. She didn't want to burden her children with
this responsibility, because they didn't really have
a relationship with Todd. We asked the administrator
of Todd's not-for-profit agency if the agency could
act as backup trustee, and the administrator agreed.
Candace, in turn, asked me to direct that upon Todd's
death, any remaining monies in the trust would go to
the not-for-profit organization.

Sometimes what seems to be the simplest course of
action actually creates a big fiasco later. Miriam's
overly simplistic planning strategy resulted in lost
assets and strained relations between her daughters.
On the other hand, by taking the bull by the horns and
educating herself about all legal options, Candace has
ensured Todd's lifetime security while also providing
for the organization that has taken care of him since
childhood. This was definitely a good outcome for
everyone involved.

Supplemental or special needs trusts should be considered by
anyone whose child or grandchild has a developmental disability,

has a cognitive impairment, or is on the autism spectrum. If one of my three children has special needs, I am not doing her any favors by leaving her one-third of my estate outright. First of all, she is probably not capable of managing the money. She might also be susceptible to influence by shady characters trying to dupe her. Finally, the monies could interfere with or prevent eligibility for any means-tested government programs to which she might otherwise be entitled.

The terms of the supplemental needs trust (SNT) allow the trustee to utilize trust assets for the benefit of the special beneficiary without disrupting his or her Medicaid, supplemental security income (SSI), or other means-tested benefits. The key with drafting this trust is to not allow the special beneficiary to receive too much. We normally say that trust assets can only be used to supplement or add to the benefits received through government programs. We forbid the trustee from making any trust distributions that could supplant or disrupt benefits. In other words, if a government program is paying rent for my son, then the trustee would not be permitted to utilize trust assets to make any rent payments. We think of SNT assets as being used for the extras in life. Permitted expenditures might be travel, entertainment, and clothing. It is recommended that the trustee purchase these items directly and then give them to the beneficiary. It is not advisable for the trustee to make a distribution of money directly to the beneficiary and then permit him to buy his own items. Having too much money in his account, for even a brief period of time, could bounce him off of a program.

There are two basic types of special needs (a.k.a. supplemental needs) trusts (SNTs). The first type is a "testamentary" trust, which is contained within your will. You do not actually fund this trust during your life. The will simply directs a certain dollar amount or percentage of the estate to be placed in the trust upon death.

The second type of SNT is an *inter vivos* trust. This refers to a trust that you create and fund during your life. Unlike a testamentary SNT, you do not have to be dead for the *inter vivos* SNT to be functional. Some of my clients prefer to set up an *inter vivos* SNT because they want to be sure that there is no delay at death that could impact the special beneficiary.

This is a personal decision. The only advice that I share with clients deciding upon which way to go is that we should avoid setting up an SNT while the special beneficiary is a minor. If you have a legal duty to support your child at the time that you establish and fund the trust, then government programs have a greater chance of laying claim to the assets.

It is sometimes necessary to establish the SNT right away if the special beneficiary comes into any money on his own. This could be the result of a personal injury lawsuit or an inheritance from a grandparent who had an unenlightened estate plan. If the special needs person is already on a government program when she comes into the windfall, then we will have to petition the court to be able to set up the trust. The court will require that the trust be created in such a way that all programs are reimbursed with any trust assets remaining upon the death of the special beneficiary. This is referred to as a "payback trust."

There is really no limit to the types of protective trusts that can be built into one's estate plan to take care of loved ones with special issues. Don't omit someone from your estate plan just because they have problems. It is far better to divide the estate into whatever percentages you wish and then specify that the shares earmarked for certain beneficiaries be held in trust and administered in accordance with whatever instructions you specify.

If, for example, a client has a fifty-four-year-old child who has not saved a cent toward retirement, I recommend that his share of the estate be held in trust. It doesn't matter to me whether his failure to save thus far was his "fault" or the result of circumstances beyond his control. One of the best predictors of future behavior is a look at one's past actions. If there are no savings by age fifty-four, I think it is a long shot, at best, that there is still time for him to create an adequate retirement nest egg. The trust is not meant as a punishment. Rather, it can be structured to pay out 5 percent per year and thereby replicate the function of a retirement plan. In addition to the 5 percent (or whatever amount you choose), the trustee could be given the discretion to make additional distributions for unexpected needs that may arise. The named trustee should, ideally, be in good health and likely able to survive the term of the trust. It is also always a good idea to name a backup trustee. If there is no ideal trustee in your life at the moment, you may wish to name two "B+" candidates who can act together as cotrustees. This arrangement provides for some built-in accountability. If one of them, for example, wants to invest in something risky, the hope is that the other trustee would caution against it. The cotrustee arrangement also enables them to share the burden. They can be given the flexibility to act separately, thereby obviating the need for both of them to take time off from work to transact trust business.

Trust arrangements are also a very good idea for beneficiaries with gambling issues, those with alcohol or other substance abuse struggles, or those who have a great track record for picking bad romantic partners. If your daughter is on husband number four, I strongly recommend that you structure her interest in your estate as a trust. Again, this is not meant to be a punishment. There is no value judgment taking place by virtue of creating the trust. You are simply taking a good look at your loved ones' current circumstances and using all available estate planning tools to enable them to receive the greatest benefit possible from your assets. Again, please resist the urge to dismiss trusts as being unnecessarily complicated. When a client says, "I'll just leave him his share, outright. If he blows it in a year, it will be his own problem. I won't be here to see it," I don't believe he truly wishes for the money to be lost, and I urge him to go home and sleep on it and come back again for another discussion.

Parenting from Beyond

By this point, I hope that you are aware that I am a strong proponent of customizing your estate plan. The outdated notion of a simple will leaving everything equally to your named beneficiaries will almost certainly fail to optimally protect them from modern-day liabilities. The question, then, is how far do we wish to go in terms of protecting our beneficiaries after we are gone? Do we wish to condition the inheritance upon the attainment of certain goals? Some of my clients are resolute in their decision to divide the estate equally and hope for the best. On the other side of the spectrum are clients who seek to govern children's behavior far into the future. A look at some of the options will hopefully enable you to decide what makes sense for your family situation.

When setting up a trust for children, grandchildren, or other beneficiaries, one may wish to avoid setting up hard rules and instead provide the trustee with some guidelines as to how you wish for the money to be used. Most of my clients want the money to be used for higher education expenses. This can be expressed as a recommendation rather than a mandate. If the trustee is given complete discretion as to how, whether, and when to make trust distributions to or for the benefit of the beneficiaries, then the assets in the trust will not be counted when the child is applying for college financial aid. If, instead, the trust required college tuition to be paid, then this would need to be disclosed on financial aid applications and would lower the amount of any award based on need.

Giving your trustee discretion over whether and how distributions are to be made will also protect the assets from any of the youngster's potential liabilities, such as a divorce. Mandated distributions to the child, on the other hand, are taken into account for property settlement purposes.

Sometimes clients are reluctant to leave all decisions up to the trustee. If, for example, the trustee is a family member, there may be a concern that the beneficiary can persuade him or her to distribute too much. These clients want to set up a more rigid mechanism to control trust assets. Depending upon the nature and extent of the conditions erected, we can expect a beneficiary to seek to have the condition thrown out by a court. Therefore, it is important to have an idea of what type of trust micromanagement will fly and what won't:

1. *Investment decisions.* A trust creator will normally give the trustee broad latitude in investment decisions. This is appropriate when you are comfortable with your named trustee. Broad latitude will enable her to deal more easily with banks,

title companies, and investment firms. If, on the other hand, you know and love your trustee but believe that her investment philosophy is not compatible with yours, then some safeguards may be in order. It is permissible to require your trustee to follow the same general asset allocation evidenced by your portfolio at the time of death. You can prohibit investments that you consider to be risky, such as commodities. You can prevent your trustee from trading "on margin" or engaging in puts and calls. It may also be a good idea to prevent your trustee from investing in something in which she has a financial interest. Let's say I name my daughter as the trustee of my grandchildren's trusts. I may wish to restrict her ability to invest in her husband's latest jerk chicken franchise idea.

2. *Conditioning receipt of the money on education benchmarks.* It is fairly common to condition receipt of an inheritance or payments from a trust on maintaining minimum grades or graduating within a certain time frame. Courts have even upheld conditions requiring a child to attend a particular college in order to collect an inheritance. Consider whether you want to require that the degree be earned within a certain period of time or if the "eight-year plan" is okay with you.

3. *Conditioning the inheritance upon getting married.* Remember Chris O'Donnell's mad pursuit of a bride in the movie *The Bachelor*? It seemed a far-fetched premise that the protagonist had twenty-four hours in which to find a wife, lest he lose a massive inheritance. In real life, though, courts have uniformly upheld marriage requirements, provided that they don't violate public policy. Requirements that a beneficiary marry someone of a given race have been uniformly tossed out by courts. By contrast, requiring a beneficiary to marry someone of a certain religion has, by and large, passed muster. What about conditioning an inheritance on a beneficiary getting divorced? Much to the dismay of some of my clients, it is not legally possible to require that a child get divorced

in order to receive an inheritance. Any condition that would tend to promote divorce is deemed to be contrary to public policy.

4. *Clean living.* It is entirely permissible to condition an inheritance upon a beneficiary staying sober or free from drugs for a certain period of time.

Conscious of the possible corrupting effect of a massive windfall, Warren Buffet famously said that he planned to leave his children with enough money that they could do anything—but not so much that they could do nothing. Parents struggling to avoid having a large inheritance sap their kids of motivation are gravitating to so-called "incentive trusts." Do you wish to encourage productivity, social consciousness, and/or savings? An incentive trust can be structured to pay a beneficiary the same amount that he earns or saves in a given year. The trust can also be structured to match or add to the annual salary of a child who has entered a noble but low-paying profession that benefits society.

Preplanning a Funeral

What on earth does this have to do with children and money? Pre-arranging a funeral can be a real gift to one's beneficiaries in several ways. By making selections ahead of time, we are relieving our loved ones from decision-making while in grief. I know firsthand that we are more inclined to overspend when selecting funeral and burial items shortly after a major loss. One result of making these decisions ahead of time will be that our loved ones have more money. By sparing them from opting for the most expensive items while grief-stricken, the family can literally save thousands of dollars. Moreover, sparing children from the miserable process of making funeral arrangements after death is a loving and thoughtful gesture. It is, for most of us, the very last action we can take that will show our children we did everything possible to shield them from needless angst and spare them from the pressures of "being sold."

Takeaways:

1. Help youngsters develop financial strength by refusing to get them everything they ask for. Children who have mastered the art of delayed gratification are more likely to become wealthy as adults.
2. Name a guardian for minor children.
3. Create a supplemental needs trust for a beneficiary with a disability.
4. Protect your kids (and grandkids) by creating minor's trusts within your estate plan.
5. Say no to relatives asking you to cosign loan agreements.
6. Consider creating a protective trust for a beneficiary with problems handling money.

7

TOXIC AGREEMENTS

So far, we have focused on love contracts and other estate planning tools and contracts that will help us preserve wealth. It is also critically important to know how to spot financially destabilizing agreements, contracts, and documents. No amount of clever lawyering can undo a "toxic contract" once entered into. In this chapter, I will attempt to sensitize you to common types of contracts that can be lethal to your future financial security and happiness.

I have always agreed with the time-honored advice that in the first year after a major loss, we shouldn't make decisions of great consequence. It is important to remember that we are in a weakened state after losing a spouse or partner. The death of a loved one results in very real physiological and psychological effects. This usually leaves us in no condition to make major decisions such as selling a home or moving out of state to live near a child. Decisions that can be put off should be. This is especially true when it comes to business dealings. Signing contracts while in a weakened state can leave us in a financially vulnerable position.

MAX'S STORY

Consider Max Miller, who lived alone following the loss of his wife, Ida. He answered the door one day to a father-and-son contracting team who made what sounded like a very reasonable proposal to him. For $25, they would climb onto his roof and spread a layer of a water-repelling polymer sealing coat. "This coating would extend the life of your roof by several years," they explained. Max felt that he had nothing to lose by accepting the offer. When the duo descended from the roof some time later, they advised Max that he had problems "up there." Max replied that the roof was only seven years old and he never experienced any trouble with it. They left him a business card in the event he had need for them in the future.

Can you guess what happened the next time it rained? Yes, Max had leaks. *They were right about the roof*, he thought. Unfortunately for Max, he was able to find the business card in the kitchen junk drawer where he tossed it. He called the "contractors" and asked them to come back to give him an estimate. They quoted $16,000 because of the "significant structural damage." Max apologized for wasting their time because he didn't have that kind of money. He owned the home and received a monthly Social Security check of $1200 but had no savings to speak of after paying for his wife's home care for the past four years.

"No problem, Mr. Miller. We can arrange the financing for you," the contractors assured. They just happened to have the needed paperwork prepared to set
it up. You see where this is going. The monthly payment for the loan was $950. Max could not possibly
afford to pay and quickly fell behind. The contractors
threatened to foreclose upon his home. Max was not a
stupid man and soon realized what had happened. He
still refused to reach out to his adult children for
help, because he felt foolish for getting into this
predicament.

Max's story had a happy ending because a suspi-
cious neighbor called the district attorney's office,
and the father-son duo eventually landed behind bars.
Today, Max is safe and sound in his home. I sometimes
shudder at the thought of the reception that a hap-
less salesperson, campaigning politician, or religious proselytizer would receive if paying a cold-call
visit to Max after this ordeal.

In many other cases, no one is alerted to the wrongdoing in time
to help.

FRANK'S STORY

Frank Eggars, a widower, came to my office to revise
his will following the loss of his wife. Seven years
after signing this will, Frank died. As the attorney for the estate, I helped the executor sort out
and pay outstanding expenses. There was one recurring
monthly expense that we couldn't make heads or tails
of. Frank was writing a monthly check in the amount of
$125, payable to TDK Inc. Looking through shoe boxes

full of old statements, we discovered a letter written
to Frank shortly after he lost his wife. The letter
advised Frank that as a member of the church choir, he
was singing songs that were protected by federal copy-
right law. Frank could be prosecuted, they claimed, if
he didn't pay a monthly licensing fee to the owners
of the copyrighted songs. And so, these scoundrels
received $125 each month for more than seven years at
their PO box. Despite efforts by law enforcement, they
were never caught.

It is never a good idea to make a deal or enter into an agreement
when you are operating from a position of weakness. If you have suffered a recent loss, or if you are temporarily low on your mojo, then
it is best to postpone entering into deals.

CINDY'S STORY

Consider Cindy, who recently lost her father. She was
thirty-six and lived at home with her parents and three
rescue cats. She helped care for her father through his
lengthy battle with lung cancer. With encouragement
from her mother and friends, Cindy decided to do something for herself for a change and booked a ticket on
a luxury cruise geared toward singles. Cindy suffered
from low self-esteem because she was morbidly obese
and had never really dated much. No bother, she wasn't
exactly looking for Mr. Right. Rather, a change of scen-
ery and unlimited dessert bars were calling her name.
    I've told more than a few people that when you
aren't looking for love, it has a habit of finding
you. Sure enough, first day on the cruise, Cindy met
a gorgeous man on line at the hot sundae bar. They hit

it off instantly. In response to her questions, Cindy
was assured that Juan-Carlos was a professional, not
married, and not an ax murderer. The next four days
were a gift from heaven. They left Cindy's stateroom
only for meals. She quickly realized that she was head
over heels in love. Cindy thought it best, though, not
to risk scaring him off with that declaration. No, she
was going to play it cool and vowed not to cry when the
ship docked. As they said their good-byes, Juan-Carlos
actually told Cindy that he was hoping to see her soon!
And he gave her a note. Cindy said that she'd save it
for later. Juan-Carlos replied that he expected payment
now. WHAT?!? Cindy tore open the envelope and found
an invoice for $2400 from an escort service. Angry and
humiliated, Cindy paid him in traveler's checks.

She came to my office to see if she could get a
refund from the escort agency. I advised her that
because the amount was over $500, the obligation must
be memorialized in writing. In other words, a verbal
agreement for goods or services in excess of $500 can
be successfully challenged by virtue of the statute of
frauds. One of the exceptions to this writing requirement, though, is when there has been "performance."
Here, despite the lack of a written agreement, Cindy
had actually paid Juan-Carlos. "But," she protested to
me, "I wasn't thinking clearly. I was stunned . . ."
My advice to Cindy was to let the matter drop, because
she faced the possibility of being charged under New
York's so-called "John Laws" with patronizing a pros-
titute. "What?!" she sputtered. I reminded her that
Juan-Carlos told her he was a "professional" during
their first conversation. She would have to admit this
under oath. Did she really want to endure the field
day that the New York tabloid newspapers would have
with this one? She let it drop—poorer but wiser.

Some of the most harmful legal documents I've seen have fallen under the category of "bad estate planning." Unfortunately, it is very common to unwittingly implement toxic estate planning.

Even experienced lawyers are capable of making life-shattering mistakes in handling their own financial affairs. When it comes to estate planning, it does not matter how smart or how well educated a person is. The input of an experienced trust and estates attorney is always recommended to spot and plan for the many "what ifs" down the road. Even estate planning attorneys should seek the input of an estate planning attorney! It is often easy to lose focus and objectivity when dealing with our own personal situations. Sometimes, seemingly straightforward issues may convince someone that they don't need to have a lawyer. While the consequences of bad "do it yourself" estate planning may take longer to manifest than those of bad DIY electrical work, the results can be just as devastating.

MARTY'S STORY

Consider the case of Judge Marty Glazer. Shortly after losing his wife, the judge asked his daughter, Alexandra, her husband, and their young son to move in with him. This would be a great way to help the young family save money and at the same time bring some life back into the big house.

Several months after the move, the judge's close friend suggested that he turn over ownership of the house to Alexandra. The rationale was that this would protect the house from his future possible long-term care claims and also avoid probate down the road. This sounded like a good idea to the judge. He and Alexandra were very close. He was absolutely confident that she would never do anything to abuse the trust he was placing in her. For her part, Alexandra viewed the transfer as a mere technicality. The whole family continued to regard the house as "Dad's."

The judge would soon learn the most important rule about estate planning: "Always expect the unexpected." Six months after his wife's funeral, the unexpected indeed occurred. Alexandra died suddenly and tragically in a car accident. This triggered a series of life-changing consequences for the judge. The first problem was that, at the tender age of thirty-four, Alexandra had not gotten around to writing her will. Ironically, she really didn't think of the house as hers and used to joke about only "owning" student loans and credit card debt. In reality though, the house was legally hers at the time of death. As mentioned earlier, without a valid will, it is up to one's state of residence to decide who receives his or her property at death. Each state has so-called "intestacy" laws, which set forth the formula by which the property is distributed. The intestate formula applied to this case gave one-half of the property to Alexandra's husband, George, and one-half to the court-appointed property guardian to hold for her four-year-old son, Andrew. (She, like Dr. Kurz in chapter 6, failed to create a minor's trust.) Judge Glazer didn't receive a penny. The house, which he had trustingly deeded over to his beloved daughter, was now under the control of his son-in-law and a court-appointed stranger. The elderly judge was left completely exposed. Talk about domestic disaster.

While still grieving over his daughter, Judge Glazer now had to worry about his own future. He got along with George, but could he really depend on him? Would George, who was still a young man, continue to let the judge live with him in the house indefinitely?

The judge decided it was time to retain a lawyer and assess his options. Unfortunately, there weren't many options to assess. His lawyer told him there was nothing that could be done to reverse the transfer of

the house. "By the way," his attorney asked, "Did you
file a gift tax return after you deeded the house to
Alexandra?"

The lawyer was correct. Whenever cash or property is transferred to another individual, the donor
(person making the gift) must file a federal gift tax
return for any amount above the gift tax exemption
limit for that year ($14,000 as of 2016). When the
deed was transferred, the annual gift tax exclusion
was $10,000, and the value of the house was $400,000.
The Judge, therefore, owed Uncle Sam 45 percent of the
value above $10,000—leaving the beleaguered retiree
with a tax bill of about $175,500.

There was another shoe poised to drop on the judge's
head: his son-in-law announced that he was ready to
start dating again. And wouldn't it be awkward to
bring any new lady friends home to find the father of
his dead wife living there? "Maybe it would be for
the best if the judge made other living arrangements."
Judge Glazer soon realized that he had no choice but
to move out of the house that was now completely owned
and controlled by other people. The now-deceased Judge
spent the last few years of his life living in his
nonwinterized summer bungalow on the East End of Long
Island.

It is also possible to jeopardize your home on account of another
person's long-term care expenses.

ROGER AND SALLY'S STORY

Roger was very close with his grandmother, Sally.
As her health worsened, it was he who ferried her

between medical appointments and in and out of the hospital. When she had a severe stroke and needed to be in a nursing home, Roger made sure that she was settled in. He cleaned out her apartment and terminated her lease agreement with the landlord. The social worker in the nursing home asked Roger if he had an elder law attorney to help the family protect some assets before applying for the Medicaid program. Sally had about $100,000 in bank accounts. After giving the matter some thought, Sally and Roger opted against sheltering any of the assets. Neither one of them thought it was right to "hide" money to get onto Medicaid. Once the money ran out, the billing office would submit a Medicaid application on behalf of Sally.

Seven years later, Roger was sued for $500,000 by the nursing home. They discovered upon Sally's death, the prior year, that no one had ever gotten around to filing the Medicaid application. The nursing home was potentially on the hook for several years of missed payments. The employee responsible for filing Medicaid applications at that time had since retired. The nursing home was about to write it off as a bad debt when they noticed the "third-party payment guarantee" in Sally's file that was signed by Roger when she was admitted.

Roger didn't recall ever signing a payment guarantee. He and his wife spent $12,000 in legal fees fighting the nursing home but lost the case anyway. The court determined that the guarantee was binding on Roger. He embarked upon a payment plan set up by the nursing home's attorneys. However, as hard as he tried, he couldn't keep up with these payments, his own mortgage, and other expenses. Roger ended up losing his home and getting divorced.

Absent a signed contractual payment obligation, no state requires that grandchildren cover the costs of a grandparent's nursing home stay. What about children? That depends upon what state you live in. Many states still have archaic so-called "filial responsibility" laws on the books, which hold children responsible for their parents' debts. These laws have been largely ignored and not enforced for decades. Recently, however, this has begun to change. In 2010, a Pennsylvania man learned this the hard way. He received a bill for nearly $100,000 for his mother's stay in a nursing home. He assumed it was a mistake that could be rectified by a phone call, but to be on the safe side, he ran it by his attorney. He learned to his shock and surprise that Pennsylvania was one of twenty-nine states that still has a filial responsibility law. His attorney assured him that he had never seen this law enforced and there should be nothing to worry about. He couldn't have been more wrong. The court was only interested in two things: Were they, in fact, parent and child? And could the child afford to pay the outstanding bill? The answer to both was a very expensive yes.

In light of Medicare's very limited (one-hundred-day) rehabilitation benefit, and the tremendous budgetary pressures that the Medicaid program imposes on states, I think it is entirely probable that we will see new teeth in the long-dormant filial responsibility laws. If you have felt that your parent's estate and long-term care planning is none of your business, think again. If you live in one of the twenty-nine filial responsibility states, you have a valid claim to a seat at your parents' planning table. You now have every right in the world to suggest that your parents look into long-term care insurance to cover the costs of any possible long-term care needed later.

Takeaways

1. After a major loss, remember that you need to assemble a trusted team around you. The team members may be an attorney, an accountant, a financial planner, a clergy member, or a relative. Please don't make any business decisions without running it past your team.

2. There are, unfortunately, some legal actions that will have to be taken within the first year of a loss. The most immediate thing we need to do is to notify Social Security. Often, the funeral director can do this for us if asked. There are also tax and financial decisions to be made. The Internal Revenue Code requires that an estate tax return be filed for the decedent no later than nine months from the date of death. We must also make certain tax elections within this time in order to prevent the entire estate from ultimately being taxed to the surviving spouse. A trip to the financial advisor is also in order to make decisions on rolling the decedent's retirement accounts over to the surviving spouse or other named beneficiary.

3. Find out whether you and/or your parents live in a state with filial responsibility laws and plan accordingly.

4. If you are ever asked to sign something for another person, please be sure that you are signing as his or her "agent" under a durable power of attorney. This way you will be personally protected. If Roger had signed the guarantee as Sally's agent, he could not have been sued personally.

5. Don't transfer your house to your kids! For many, this seems like a simple way to avoid probate, reduce estate taxes, and protect the home against long-term-care claims. In reality, transferring home ownership will likely to do more harm than good. Even absent the statistically rare twist of fate experienced by Judge Glazer, there still would have been problems caused by transferring the property to Alexandra. Here's why:

    - *Property taxes.* Any property tax discounts that you receive because you're a senior, a veteran, or a veteran's widow will be lost once you sign the deed of your house over to your children.

    - *Children's liabilities.* Once ownership is transferred to your kids, the house is completely vulnerable to their legal misfortunes. If Alexandra had lived long enough to learn for herself what a jerk George was, she probably would have left him. He could have then laid claim to one-half of the home's value in a divorce proceeding. The same holds true for other types of claims and liabilities including bankruptcy, judgment creditors, or lawsuits. The property could also count against a grandchild who may apply for college financial aid in the future.

- *Capital gains.* When an asset is worth more today than it was at the time of purchase, it has built-in "capital gains," which are taxed upon sale. When someone sells his or her primary residence, up to $250,000 of capital gains is forgiven by virtue of the Internal Revenue Code (Section 121). A husband and wife together can have up to $500,000 forgiven. When someone makes a completed lifetime gift of appreciated property, the new owner takes the property with the donor's purchase price (basis) as the new floor to measure gain. Children most often do not qualify to take the $250,000 capital gains exclusion, because it is usually not their primary residence. In our example, if Alexandra didn't predecease her father and sold the house at his death, she would have had to pay federal and state capital gains taxes on the difference between her parents' purchase price in the 1950s (say, $50,000) and the ultimate sale price. If she could demonstrate that she lived there for two of the past five years prior to the sale, she would have qualified for the $250,000 exclusion, thereby elevating her cost basis to $300,000. If the sale price were $575,000, then $325,000 would have still been subject to capital gains tax.

6. Some people try to cleverly get around the capital gains rule by "selling" the house to children for $10. The Internal Revenue Code provides for this gimmick by treating the transaction as "part sale part gift." The children's basis, when calculating gain in a future sale, would be $50,010.

7. What about a real sale to children at fair market value? This would put $575,000 into the parents' bank account ,which would then be exposed to long-term care and possibly estate tax consequences.

8

TRUSTS AS LOVE CONTRACTS

"Put not your trust in money, but put your money in trust," counseled Oliver Wendell Holmes Sr. more than one hundred years ago. I think of trusts as love contracts to the extent that they are legal structures whose chief purpose is to protect assets for the benefit of our loved ones and ourselves. An ideal trust, like any of the love contracts, will protect assets *for* our loved ones and ourselves while simultaneously protecting assets *from* our loved ones and their problems—provided, of course, that we know how to select the right trust.

Employing the love contracting model to the trust selection process, we must first be clear about what it is we wish to accomplish. Do we wish to reduce the estate tax bite for our children, protect assets in the event long-term care is needed, keep money from being lost to a beneficiary's liabilities, or merely wish to avoid probate? Once we know what we wish to accomplish, we can determine what, exactly, we are willing to do and what we are unwilling to do in order to get there. Applied to the selection of trusts, this threshold analysis will center on what level of protection we want and what degree of control we are willing and unwilling to give up in that process.

Let's look at a few different types of trusts, the first of which does not require us to give up any control.

Revocable Trust

If you've ever attended a living trust seminar, you may wonder why everyone doesn't have one. The concept is very appealing. The creator can serve as his or her own trustee. Full control over the assets in the trust is retained. There is no need to go to a third party in order to access the trust. The primary purpose of this type of trust is that it will avoid probate at death. Assets in a revocable trust pass automatically to one's beneficiaries.

Many people mistakenly think that if they have a will in place, their beneficiaries will not be subjected to a lengthy probate proceeding in court. A related misimpression is that if one avoids probate, then he or she somehow avoids paying estate taxes at death.

The reality is that every one of us should have a will, but the goal is not to have to use it. Any asset that must pass according to the terms of one's will goes to probate. What assets, then, need to pass through one's will? Anything without a named beneficiary or surviving joint owner. As between a husband and wife, we normally don't need to probate the will of the first to die, because the surviving spouse is almost always listed on all accounts as the beneficiary and on all real estate as the joint owner. Upon the death of the second spouse, however, children are often subjected to probate because there are usually assets that fail to name beneficiaries or a joint owner.

What exactly is probate? It is the court-supervised process by which the terms of one's will are carried out. A will is not "self-activating" or automatic. If, for example, a will names me as my mother's sole beneficiary, I can't simply bring the will to the bank and expect them to hand over my mother's accounts. The bank will ask for two things: my mother's death certificate and the court's certificate of appointment or "letter testamentary." We can only get this court document after the judge is satisfied that the will itself is valid, that it was properly executed, and that the decedent had the capacity to make the will. The process by which the court makes these inquiries is called probate. Probate also requires notification to all of the people who would inherit your assets if you didn't do a will. These are one's "heirs at law." If I were to die without a will and am survived by a husband and children, state law provides that my husband receive one-half of my assets and my children receive the remaining one-half. If there is any complexity within the family, or if the will is problematic in any way, then we can expect a long, drawn-out process. A homemade or "do it yourself" will is often subject to greater court scrutiny and will therefore result in a lengthier probate process for my beneficiaries. There are several legal documents that can effectively be done without an attorney. The will, however, is not one of them.

If one's will is created by an attorney, there is a presumption under state law that it is valid. This goes a long way toward speeding up the probate process. Even though I have created many thousands of wills for my clients over the years and could probably write one in my sleep, I did not write my own will. Another attorney wrote my will so that if there is a need for probate, the process will be as short as possible, and my family won't be subjected to a drawn-out court proceeding. Even though we are able to streamline the court process with a good will, it is still a court process, which is a matter of public record. It is the ultimate airing of one's dirty laundry. This is how newspapers are able to report on the value of dead celebrities' estates, who got what, and who was cut out. The reporter can simply request the probate file from the county Surrogate's Court and snoop away.

The probate process can also be very costly. There are steep court filing fees and hefty legal fees charged to probate a will. I know attorneys who rely on the future probate of wills they've written as an important element of their own financial retirement planning!

Given the lack of privacy, expenses, and delays involved, it is always a good idea to try to avoid probate entirely.

The revocable trust does effectively avoid probate for the assets that it contains. So why doesn't everyone have a revocable trust? What, if any, are the downsides? There are two that I can think of. The first is when someone actually forgets to transfer assets into the trust. In addition to listing the assets in the trust, we must literally go to the bank or brokerage firm and transfer the assets into the trust. If real estate is involved, then we must in fact change the deed and have it recorded at the County Clerk's office. Having a living or revocable trust without changing legal ownership of one's assets is a waste of the paper that the trust was printed on. It is a legal "nullity." There have been several lawsuits against nonattorney document companies alleging failure to inform the consumer that any action was needed after the trust was purchased. Simply having the revocable trust will not avoid probate if it is not the legal owner of one's assets.

The other downside of a revocable trust is when someone mistakenly believes that it can do more than simply avoid probate. I have seen unscrupulous or uninformed attorneys and nonattorney document sellers give the impression that a living or revocable trust can in and of itself protect a family's assets. Common sense and federal law tell us otherwise. Think about it—if I have total access to and control over my assets in the revocable trust, how can I then turn around and expect a nursing home or other creditor to consider the assets unavailable?

ALICE AND DAVE'S STORY

Alice Walker's son, Dave, suggested that she give her home to him in order to protect it from future possible long-term care costs. He advised her that the so-called Medicaid look-back period is now five years. If she gave him the house now, it would be "invisible" to long-term care claims in five years. Having heard horror stories from friends, Alice was not about to do this. Some time later, she and her friend Mary attended a seminar presented by a local attorney,

Wayne Winkler, touting the virtues of "living revocable trusts." Initially enticed by the free refresh-
ments, she and Mary attended. The charismatic attorney advised the group that a living revocable trust
protected assets from probate, taxes, and long-term
care expenses without any loss of control over the
house and other assets. Alice was interested enough
to schedule a private consultation with the attorney.
When he went through the list of benefits again, Alice
asked if he would be willing to state in writing that
she would not lose any control over the assets in the
trust. He promised to include that guarantee in the
retainer agreement he sent her.

When Alice received the retainer agreement, she was
impressed that Mr. Winkler did guarantee that she would
remain in total control. She was less impressed with
the $3700 legal fee quoted. The letter was promptly
filed in the dining room breakfront "limbo" drawer and
was never taken back out. Mary, on the other hand, went
ahead with Mr. Winkler's proposal. Over the course of
several weeks, Mary executed the trust and transferred
her home and bank accounts into it.

Fortunately for Alice, she was up late one night
and saw an infomercial selling do-it-yourself living revocable trusts for $49.99. This time she was
ready to pull the trigger. She put down the ice cream
bowl, picked up the phone, and bought her trust. It
arrived several days later. Alice signed where indicated and stored it in a strongbox with her will and
other important papers. She virtuously assured her
son, Dave, that she had taken care of the estate planning and he would be spared the delays of probate and
the expenses of long-term care and estate taxes.

Three years later, Alice died. When Dave then tried
to sell the house as sole beneficiary of the trust, he

learned from the buyer's title company that the deed had
never been transferred into the trust. They would now
have to probate the will after all. This meant tracking
down his estranged brother, Jimmy, who was last seen
hitchhiking to Haight-Ashbury in '69. The Surrogate's
Court judge appointed a guardian ad litem to help search
for him. Two years later, Dave was finally able to sell
the house. After satisfying the back taxes, utilities,
and lien on the house for Alice's long-term care, he
didn't walk away with much at all.

Was Mary better off because she created her living revocable trust
with a lawyer? Let's see.

MARY'S STORY

Six years after creating her trust with Mr. Winkler,
Mary required nursing home care. She quickly exhausted
the limited Medicare rehabilitation benefit of one
hundred days. The billing office asked her daughter
Nancy if there was a long-term care insurance policy
in place. Nancy said there was none and told the billing office that she wished to apply for Medicaid for
her mother. After providing the nursing home's Medicaid coordinator with all requested financial information, she was told to come back after exhausting all
of the assets in the trust. What?!

"My mother paid $3700 to have that done six years
ago. The look-back period of five years has passed.
Please look at this again," asked Nancy. The coordinator broke the news to Nancy that because the assets
in the trust were 100 percent available to Mary at all
times, her look-back period never did begin to run at

all. For Medicaid purposes, it was as if Mary had done
no planning at all. After confirming the bad news with
another attorney, Nancy proceeded to sell the house
and use the money to pay for the nursing home. When
Mary died four years later, there was $10,000 left to
be divided between the children.

Another benefit of the revocable trust, according to promoters, is that it will provide for continuity of decision-making activities in the event that the creator becomes unable to handle his own affairs. It is true that by naming a backup or successor trustee, there will be someone empowered to step in and act if the primary trustee is physically or mentally incapacitated. Remember, however, that the trustee only has control over and access to assets that are actually in the trust. There may be many assets that aren't in the trust. Moreover, one's backup trustee would not be empowered to transact business with the IRS, social security, insurance companies, etc. If continuity of your business and financial dealings is the primary motivation to create a revocable trust, you may be better off relying on a good power of attorney (see chapter 13).

Assets in one's revocable trust are also fully countable for tax purposes. Any asset that I have retained access to (even if it is only an income interest) will be included in my gross taxable estate at death. It is very important to remember that assets do not avoid estate tax just because they may avoid probate. If this were the case, it would be so simple to avoid paying taxes that the government wouldn't collect any! If you have any goal in addition to merely avoiding probate, then you should become acquainted with some of the other trust types.

Estate Tax Trust

This is a type of irrevocable trust that is useful for an individual or family with assets above the applicable state and federal estate tax thresholds. Just as we pay income taxes to the state and federal government every April, we may be subject to two levels of estate taxes at death. As of this writing, the federal estate tax exemption is $5.4 million per person. Any assets below this level will not be subject to federal estate taxation. Many states have eliminated their separate estate taxes. To check your state's current estate tax status, go to www.mylawyerann.com.

Any assets in excess of the lesser of the state and federal tax thresholds should, ideally, be owned by an estate tax trust. This can remove the assets from one's gross taxable provided that the trust is properly structured. The most common drafting pitfall with this type of trust is to allow the creator or "settlor" to retain any income interest in the trust assets. The Internal Revenue Code specifically states that assets with a retained income interest are includible in the estate tax base. The creator must also relinquish all legal control over and rights to the assets transferred into the estate tax trust. This can be off-putting to many people.

If, for example, I were to transfer my home into an estate tax trust but then continue to live there, then the entire fair market value of the house would be subject to estate taxation upon my death. It would, however, be possible for me to rent the house from the trust. This would not violate the terms of the trust. Moreover, any payment of rent from me to the trust would have the added benefit of removing these monies from my taxable estate.

Life Insurance Trust

This is a variation of the basic estate tax trust, which is designed to keep life insurance death benefits from being taxed. Many people are surprised to learn that the life insurance death benefit is subject to estate tax. Insurance salespeople never fail to mention the tax-free aspect of life insurance. However, life insurance is only free of income taxes, not estate taxes. By creating a life insurance trust and changing the ownership of my policy into the trust, the payout upon death will avoid estate taxation.

The life insurance trust can also include provisions to protect beneficiaries from a windfall payout that they may not be prepared to handle. It is often a big mistake to name one's spouse as the direct beneficiary on life insurance. If my surviving spouse develops dementia or any other type of long-term illness, these assets could evaporate quickly. Moreover, if he remarries, it will then be quite unlikely that my own children will receive any benefit from these assets upon his subsequent death. Naming my children as direct beneficiaries is also inadvisable. This is especially true if any of the children has a developmental disability, substance-abuse issue, bad marriage track record, or over-spending issues. The trust can provide my beneficiaries with generous benefits without subjecting the assets to their liabilities.

Asset Protection Trust

This trust type allows for more flexibility than the estate tax–type trust. If we are not dealing with a taxable estate because your assets are below the current threshold, but you still wish to protect assets such as your home from probate as well as liabilities such as long-term care expenses, then this trust may be an attractive option.

The asset protection trust (APT) is technically irrevocable. Remember that the revocable or living trust only avoids probate. If we are seeking any type of liability protection from external threats or internal (family) threats to our wealth, then we need to consider an irrevocable trust. The APT is not, however, as restrictive as the estate tax trust types. It is only considered irrevocable because I, acting alone, cannot get mad at the world and pull all of my stuff out of the trust. I can, however, tell my trustee what I think he or she should do with trust assets. This may be putting a new roof on my home, buying a new television, or purchasing a car. What can I do if the trustee says no? If the trust is properly drafted, I can *fire* the trustee who is annoying me and replace her with a new trustee. I cannot act as my own trustee, because then the APT would morph into a living or revocable trust. I can, however, retain the ability to remove and replace my trustee whenever I wish. Provided that I was given that power by the terms of the trust, I can fire the trustee for any reason, or no reason at all. What if my named trustee is traveling and I want to sell a trust asset? Then I will temporarily replace her with another trustee until she returns.

An added power that we can retain with the APT is the ability to change the named beneficiaries. Circumstances change, relationships change, and people change. It is very nice to know that you can still react to life's curveballs long after the trust has been created. If, for example, I create a trust to own my house and name my three children as beneficiaries and a child predeceases me, it is very important to be able to move that child's share, either to his surviving children or to my two remaining children. It is often advisable to prevent my widowed daughter-in-law from receiving my son's share. Otherwise, she could remarry and potentially lose the money to her new spouse.

Retaining the power to change the beneficiaries will also enable me to change the percentages that my children will ultimately receive.

Let's say that Peggy created a trust to own her home and named her children, Ellen and Steve, as the equal beneficiaries. As years go by, Peggy comes to rely more and more upon Ellen. She lives closer, visits her mother regularly, takes her to appointments, and does errands. Steve, on the other hand, is perfectly lovely to Peggy when she sees him. The only problem is that this happens only about twice a year. He is on his third marriage and is very busy with his new family. Should Peggy reconsider leaving equal distributions to her children? My clients are split on this issue. There are certainly valid arguments that can be made either way. The only matter of critical importance to me is that Peggy has the power to make that change. Whether she decides to increase Ellen's share or not is ultimately her judgment call. My only role here is to have drafted the trust properly at the outset, so that she is able to make any change she may wish to make in the future.

The chief functions of the APT are to avoid probate and protect one's assets in the event that long-term care is later needed. There is currently a five-year "look back" period on transfers to any individual or entity other than a spouse. In order to commence the running of this clock (after which the assets are exempt for Medicaid purposes), the trust must be irrevocable. However, because it does not have to be quite so restrictive as the estate tax trust, the creator or grantor may retain lifetime ownership rights over a house, condo, or co-op that may be owned by the trust. One's property tax exemptions, step-up in tax basis (elimination of capital gains) at death, and $250,000 capital gains exclusion on the sale of a primary residence during life ($500,000 for a couple) can all be preserved with a properly drafted asset protection trust.

If you get the impression that I am a big fan of trusts, you are right. I believe that only a small minority of us is adequately served by a simple will alone. Answer the following questions to determine how a trust may make sense and which types may be appropriate for your situation:

1. Do you have a child or other beneficiary who has difficulty handling finances? Is this the result of a developmental disability or long-term illness? If so, a supplemental needs trust should be considered. If the difficulty is the result of a gambling problem, substance-abuse problem, or chronic overspending, then a spendthrift trust may make sense.

2. Has your spouse or significant other been diagnosed with a dementia-type illness? Consider creating an asset protection trust to hold legal title to your home. This will ensure that he has a roof over his head if he survives you, while also protecting the asset vis-à-vis long-term care expenses and his possible subsequent marriages.

3. Do you have a child who is estranged from the family? Any of the trusts, including a revocable trust, will enable your remaining beneficiaries to avoid a long, drawn-out probate process. Again, you are not required to leave anything to a child (except in Louisiana), but the court will not allow your will to be probated until it tracks down the missing child to give him or her the opportunity to challenge the will.

4. Do you wish to leave more to one child? This may be because they need it more or deserve it more. It is usually advisable to leave the "extra distribution" to one child by way of a separate trust naming him or her as sole beneficiary This way, the main will or trust can recite an "equal distribution" so that no one's feelings are hurt.

5. Are you an older parent? Those of us who started or added to
   our families later in life need to pay special care to ensuring
   that children are protected upon our passing. For most of us,
   this means a descendant's trust with a staggered distribution
   (25/30/35). This protects our children to the greatest extent
   possible from poor decisions or liabilities like divorce. Note
   that this trust can be used for college and other expenses
   prior to the stated distribution ages.
6. Are you in a second marriage? Those of us who wish to provide for a surviving second spouse without disinheriting our
   children may wish to consider a bypass trust. This can be
   used to hold all or some assets for the benefit of a surviving spouse and then redirect them to our children upon the
   death of the survivor.

Irrevocable Is Not as Scary as It Sounds

Many people understandably have a strong negative visceral response
to the word Irrevocable. It does sound frightening. None of us wants
to be locked into a situation that we may wish to change later on.
The good news, though, is that there are several ways to change an
irrevocable trust in the event that you wish to do so in the future.

The best way to preserve your future "maneuverability" is to
build it into the trust document when you create it. It is true that
one may not retain access to or control over the assets transferred
into a trust if the goal is to avoid estate tax. One can, however, retain
the right to remove and replace the trustee. This is an important
power for psychological reasons. By virtue of my retained ability to
remove and replace my trustee, I don't feel that I am "stuck" with a
bad trustee. We all know that life and relationships change. This is
why I always recommend that my clients retain the ability to make
this change in the future.

An added benefit of being able to remove and replace the trustee is
that this power will enable the trust to qualify for so-called "grantor"

trust status under the Internal Revenue Code. This means that the trust will be disregarded for income tax purposes. If trust assets earn income, then that income can still be reported on my personal 1040 income tax return. This type of trust does not have to have its own income tax return prepared.

Another element of flexibility that can be built into the trust has to do with income distribution. Again, one may not retain an income interest in the trust if the goal is to avoid estate tax inclusion of trust assets. One can, however, allow the trustee discretion to give income to certain of your beneficiaries, including a spouse, provided that certain conditions are met.

Often, I am asked to review poorly drafted trusts that don't provide any "wiggle room." Depending upon the circumstances, we may still be able to modify even irrevocable trusts by virtue of state law.

Statutory Reformation

We can often reform irrevocable trusts without going to court by virtue of a state law that allows the settlor, upon written consent of all those beneficially interested in the trust property, to amend or revoke a trust in whole or in part. This relief is not available if any beneficiary is unwilling or unable to give consent. If, for example, a beneficiary is a minor or is under a disability, or, in the case of a testamentary trust (created by one's will), the Grantor has died, then statutory reformation will not be of use.

If statutory reformation relief is unavailable, certain trust terms may still be changed by "decanting." Every state now has a decanting law that allows a trustee to move assets from an existing trust into a new trust with more favorable terms. The decanting process is a bit more cumbersome than reformation, but it is very useful when a beneficiary refuses or is unable to sign off on the change needed.

A typical situation requiring a decanting remedy is an existing trust for the benefit of a minor. These were often (inadvisably) scheduled to terminate upon the child reaching eighteen, at which point she received all of the money or other assets outright. If I wish to prevent the eighteen-year-old from coming into this windfall, I can create a new trust with a longer term and have the trustee of the existing trust "decant," or "pour," some or all of the trust assets into the new trust. Reformation would probably not be a realistic option in this situation, because it requires the beneficiary to give written consent. Would the typical eighteen-year-old willingly agree to postpone receipt of money for five or more years? I have to think that if the child is willing, then he is in the small minority of eighteen-year-olds who might not need to be protected from their own spendthrift ways in the first place. Even so, I would still counsel that the trust term be extended so that the trust payout doesn't prevent eligibility for any means-tested college financial aid programs. The extension can also keep these assets safe from an ill-advised early marriage or other liabilities.

Decanting relief, though greatly expanded in recent years, is still not available to all trusts. Many state statutes exclude trustees with a present or future beneficial interest in the trust from being able to decant. This prohibition renders decanting relief unavailable to countless trusts that name the settlor's child or other loved one as both a trustee and ultimate remainder beneficiary.

Court-Ordered Reformation

This allows a party to an existing trust to petition the court for a change one wishes to make. The power of the Surrogate's Court to reform (even "irrevocable") trusts rests in the court's inherent equitable powers. In the case of a drafting error or change in circumstance, the court will attempt to ascertain and then effectuate the intent of the settlor.

Let's say my father created a trust for the benefit of all of his children and grandchildren. The trust is scheduled to terminate upon the tenth anniversary of his death, at which point each child and grandchild receives his or her share of the trust directly. If I am the named trustee of this trust, I would be powerless to hold back the share of any beneficiary who is, for any reason, ill prepared to receive money. Absent some wiggle room built into the trust document when it was drafted, all I can do, as the trustee, is follow the trust directions. This is so, even if my sister's daughter has recently been diagnosed with severe autism. It would be a disaster if I had to actually pay the required distribution to my niece. She is unable to deal with finances, and these monies would render her ineligible for means-tested government benefits that she is receiving. What legal remedies are available?

Statutory (DIY) reformation would not be available here because the grantor or creator of the trust (my father) is deceased and is therefore unable to give the written consent required by law. Decanting would, similarly, not be available. This is because I am the trustee and I am also an ultimate beneficiary of the trust. Wearing these two hats is usually not a problem in other situations, but it will render decanting unavailable.

Only through a petition to the court can I ask the judge to allow my niece's assets to be held in a supplemental needs trust for her lifetime benefit. I can argue that the creator of the trust could not have known that any of the beneficiaries would have a special circumstance preventing them from having money. (*Note: I would argue to the court loudly and persuasively that my father could not have known about a special circumstance and, for that reason, failed to address it in the trust. However, when I work with clients, I urge them to imagine any number of wacky life events that may come to pass. This is why we want to build maximum flexibility into all of our documents.*)

Takeaways

1. Avoid DIY estate planning.
2. A living revocable trust does not protect one dime from either estate taxes or long-term care costs. Common sense tells us that if the assets are 100 percent available to us, then they are also available to our creditors (IRS and nursing homes).
3. Irrevocable trusts are not as scary as they sound—*if they are drafted properly.*

9

SECOND-MARRIAGE PLANNING

Love may be lovelier—but it is also a whole lot more complicated the second time around. The divorce rate for second marriages is approximately 60 percent. When we are older, we have fewer working years ahead to recover from being financially devastated in a divorce. Therefore, going without a prenup should not even be an option. Also, in a second marriage, the parties are likely to have separate children. It is critically important to discuss your financial obligations to your ex-spouses and children from prior relationships ahead of time. If your household finances will be seriously affected, you deserve to know this and plan for it ahead of time.

One of the big financial bones of contention specific to second marriages has to do with support expectations to the parties' respective adult children. How will it impact your household budget if your husband-to-be pays for his daughter's upcoming (third) wedding? What about bailing out a child whose home is on the verge of foreclosure? Paying for grandchildren's college tuition? You should also discuss your feelings about cosigning mortgage or other loan applications for family members. This will affect both of you, because the mere act of cosigning will negatively affect the guarantor's credit score. This, in turn, will trigger financial consequences in your own lives. It is much better to get these issues out on the table in advance rather than be surprised in the future.

Another key legal issue in second-marriage planning is how the new spouse should be provided for at death. The competing interests here are typically one's adult children and the new spouse. There is an expectation on the part of adult children that assets accumulated in the first marriage will, in some measure, inure to the benefit of the children of that marriage.

Those in a second marriage should avoid "plain vanilla" wills at all costs. It is a very common mistake to make a will leaving everything to your new spouse or, in the event that they predecease you, to your adult children. At first glance, this appears to take care of both the new spouse and the adult children, but this is not the case.

JACK AND LINDSAY'S STORY

Consider Jack (fifty-seven) and Lindsay (fifty-three). They each came into the marriage with two adult children, whose only point of agreement was that their parents' marriage was a horrible idea. Shortly after the wedding, Jack's personal trainer suggested that he redo his will, based on his mistaken belief that his ex-wife, Sandy, would otherwise have a claim to Jack's assets. Jack's nephew, though still in law school, offered to do the will, because he had access to a template in one of his textbooks. The will provided that upon Jack's death, everything went to Lindsay.

If Lindsay predeceased Jack, then everything would go to Jack's children, Jacqueline and Jayson. Four years later, Jack suffered a fatal fall from the newly constructed rock-climbing wall at his gym. In accordance with the terms of the will, Lindsay inherited everything. This included not only the house but also all personal property, such as photo albums, diplomas, awards, books, and other sentimental items. During Jack's life, Lindsay tried to keep a lid on her true feelings for his kids. Now, she was determined to settle some scores, and she made it her business to never let Jacqueline or Jayson have anything of their father's. This included the settlement proceeds of Lindsay's lawsuit against the gym for Jack's conscious pain and suffering after landing on an elliptical trainer moments prior to his death. Upon Lindsay's death, where do you think all of the assets will go? My educated guess is that they will go to her children and/or to some new boyfriend or husband. I can almost guarantee that Jacqueline and Jayson will receive nothing.

Jack never intended for Lindsay to receive everything and for his children to get nothing. What could he have done differently? He could have created a marital bypass trust for Lindsay's lifetime benefit. This could have been funded with all or some of Jack's assets upon his death. The trust is designed so that the surviving spouse receives all of the income that the assets generate every year. In addition to the income, the trust could also have given Lindsay a fixed annual percentage of principal. The named trustee would also have discretion to give Lindsay more, in the event of a real need. Then, upon the death of Lindsay, this trust could have directed all remaining trust assets to Jacqueline and Jayson. Needless to

say, it is always best to avoid naming children as the
trustees of this type of trust. The inherent conflict
of interest results in investments that throw off little or no actual income in favor of long-term internal
asset appreciation, which inures to the benefit of
themselves as the ultimate beneficiaries.

If Jack had wanted Lindsay to receive everything,
then his planning actions would have accomplished this
purpose. Except for Louisiana, no state gives children
a legal right to be provided for in a will.

How should the planning have been structured if
Jack didn't wish for Lindsay to receive anything? Perhaps Lindsay is independently wealthy and doesn't need
any portion of Jack's estate. It is often the case in
a second marriage to keep the assets totally separate
during life in order to provide for the parties' own
children at death.

If, for whatever reason, you do not wish to provide for a surviving spouse at death, then one of the love contracts is necessary. Without a valid prenup or postnup, the laws of every state will provide
the widowed spouse with generous estate rights—even if he or she
isn't named in the will. Absent an explicit written waiver, a surviving
spouse is entitled to the greater of $50,000 or one-third of the entire
estate. The only asset not counted for purposes of calculating this
"elective share" is life insurance. Every other asset, whether passing
through the will or directly to a named beneficiary, will be counted.
For example, if an estate worth $900,000 consists of a 401K of
$400,000 and CDs of $500,000 and adult children are the named
beneficiaries, the surviving spouse can lay claim to $300,000 of the
assets, even though he or she is not named as a beneficiary.

If you do not wish for a new spouse to lay claim to estate assets,
these rights must be waived within a valid prenup or postnup. This is
true even though you may have given each other your solemn promise not to make legal estate claims later. Consider that it is often the

surviving spouse's children who instigate these claims. If you wish to avoid "blended family warfare," you must have appropriate legal agreements in place.

Living arrangements upon death or breakup must also be hammered out in a second marriage situation. This is because the primary residence is commonly titled in one party's name. Upon breakup or death, will the nonowner be financially able to secure adequate replacement living arrangements? If not, a financial provision should be included within the love contract for this purpose.

The most common (but imperfect) way to deal with the housing problem upon death is to grant the nonowner survivor a so-called "life estate" in the home. The goal here is to provide a roof over the head of the surviving spouse, and then upon his or her subsequent death, the home will revert to the adult children (or other estate beneficiaries) of the first to die. This approach makes intuitive sense but often has unintended consequences.

A life estate for the survivor quite literally means that he or she is the de facto owner until death. The family would, therefore, be unable to sell the home or otherwise use it regardless of whether the survivor gets remarried, moves away, or winds up in a nursing home for years. To add insult to injury, the nursing home would be entitled to require that the property be rented out and the income used toward the survivor's care.

A better solution would be to create a trust that grants the surviving spouse a "right of occupancy" in the house. With this, we can specify events in addition to death that will have the legal effect of terminating the survivor's right to reside in the property. For example, the right of occupancy might terminate upon the earlier of the survivor's death, remarriage, voluntary departure, or absence from the property for a continuous period in excess of four months. This specificity will prevent the adult children from being stuck with an asset that they can't sell or otherwise use. It is also critically important that the love contract and will or trust creating the right of occupancy clearly spell out who is responsible for what expenses.

Second marriages usually involve people who, in the words of Peter Pan's Wendy, are "ever so much more than twenty." The good news here is that we are living longer today than ever before. This also means, though, that we are more likely to develop some cranky medical problems that our grandparents didn't live long enough to experience. Planning for long-term care in the context of a second marriage is essential. Specifically, we need to give some thought to two major issues: Who will be in charge of our care plans, and who will be responsible for paying for long-term care? The whole point of doing advance planning is so we can decide, for ourselves, how any needed care will be delivered.

Paying for this care is a challenge for millions of families in this country. In the context of our current national dialogue and debates over health-care reform, long-term care is not even being discussed. It is truly the elephant in the room. As it stands now, Medicare, together with a Medicare-supplement policy, will do a great job of covering primary medical care (doctor's office) and acute care in a hospital for those sixty-five and over. Beyond this, coverage is very limited. You may have noticed that over the course of the past twenty years or so, hospitals keep us for a much shorter period of time than they used to. I can remember my grandmother going to the hospital once a year for "tests." She remained there for about a week. It was sort of like a poor woman's trip to a spa. This has changed dramatically. Because of the way hospitals are now paid, they are looking to get us out from the moment we are admitted. These "quicker and sicker" discharges routinely result in a stay in a rehabilitation facility. At "rehab," Medicare and the supplement will cover "up to" one hundred days. Beyond this, "the rubber meets the road," and we are personally responsible to pay for this care, both for ourselves as well as our spouse. The laws of every state impose a spousal payment responsibility in the context of nursing home care. I have seen people wiped out because of the expense of a spouse's nursing home bills (which in New York City can easily exceed $15,000 per month!).

To prevent a nursing home financial tsunami, couples contemplating a second marriage can do a few things: if you qualify, consider purchasing long-term care insurance (see chapter 13). This can protect your nest eggs and also reduce blended family resentment arising from the prospect of hoped-for inheritances being used for a new spouse's nursing home bills.

Another way to avoid a nursing home financial catastrophe is to avoid a nursing home. This is best accomplished by way of your personal long-term care plan, which emphasizes care within your home.

If the care needed involves the nonglamorous functions of life such as feeding, bathing, dressing, and toileting, this can usually be provided at home. If a plan is put in place ahead of time, we maximize our chances of receiving future needed care in our own homes. This is preferable to a nursing home for many reasons. The cost of home care is a fraction of care in a nursing home. Moreover, many experts asked will agree that medical outcomes are better if a patient remains in his own home. One's familiar surroundings are a source of comfort, particularly for those with cognitive impairments. Depression, bedsores, incontinence, and infections are just a few examples of medical problems that can be worsened by placement in an institutional setting.

None of us wants to end up in a nursing home. The image of life in a typical nursing home is sobering. Imagine the continuous smell of urine in the air and being cared for by people who don't remember your name. You could find yourself sharing a room with a stranger who screams all night. The food is horrible, a television blares reruns all day, and you are forced to play bingo three days a week.

When asked, 99 percent of my clients tell me that they would prefer to receive long-term care in their own homes. However, without a plan in place ahead of time, chances to return home following hospitalization are lower. Following an initial rehab stint, any additional stay will be in the custodial care or nursing home area of the same facility. This level of care tends to provide far less to the patient. The caregiver-to-patient ratio is lower, and there is much less stimulation. With a lower level of sensory input, cognitive impairments can worsen. With less attention from caregivers, the individual is more likely to become incontinent. Make no mistake about it: the longer a person is in a facility, the less likely it is that they will be able to return home. Without a home-care plan put in place in advance of the crisis, a delay is inevitable. Crisis planning is never optimal. Short tempers and differences of opinion between family members can cause delays in getting home care in place and ready for the patient to return.

Inevitably, someone in the family suggests that they delay Mom's return home for "just a month" until everything is put into place. The sad reality for many is that Mom will be much less able to come home after a month or more in the nursing home following rehab.

What can we do ahead of time to increase our chances of returning home? Let your family and primary care physician know that this is what you want. A frank discussion with the individual that you have appointed as agent under your health-care proxy (this form can be downloaded from www.myelderlawattorney.com) will go a long way.

You can also declare your intention to remain at home within your living will by adding the following language to it: "Should I require personal needs assistance, it is my intention to have this care provided to me in my own home unless it is medically or otherwise impracticable."

Taking a few steps in advance of a crisis will go far to protect your nest egg and your happiness.

Takeaways

1. Second-marriage planning should include investigating long-term care payment sources so that you aren't wiped out by a new spouse's future possible nursing home bills.
2. Arrange for the surviving spouse to have a roof over his or her head upon the death of the homeowner. We want to stop short of giving the survivor full ownership of the residence, however, if our goal is for adult children to eventually inherit it.
3. If you wish for adult children to be provided for at your death, then avoid naming a new spouse as the sole beneficiary under your will or trust. Instead, consider establishing a trust for the lifetime benefit of a surviving spouse, which directs that everything remaining upon her death revert to your adult children.

10

THE INTERNAL LAWS OF LOVE AND MONEY

We have looked at external threats to wealth such as taxes, con artists, break-ups, and long-term care costs. There are also internal forces at work that can powerfully determine whether we attract and build wealth or repel it—even before the evil outsiders can try to take it away.

Before embarking upon a love contract or any other legal planning, I believe it is important to do some internal work in the form of a "solo love contract" (SLC) to increase our capacity to build and keep wealth while simultaneously removing obstacles in its path. The solo love contract resembles a New Year's resolution but produces more effective results by utilizing an actual contract process. It may seem odd at first to enter into a contract with oneself. Think about it, though—whose actions are we more able to directly influence and control than our own? By learning how to effectively manage ourselves and commit, in writing, to doing so, we can powerfully ensure that our efforts will directly boost our personal wealth-building power.

Thus far, we have seen many examples of people compromising their future personal security and happiness because they agreed to something they shouldn't have. A common theme running through each bad decision is that every person who was "had" was not dealing from a position of power. They all either lacked sufficient knowledge to properly evaluate and anticipate the consequences of their actions, or their power was low as a result of a recent loss or other personal roadblock. No one should enter into any business dealing or personal collaboration when operating from a position of weakness. What kinds of decisions do we make when we lack sufficient knowledge about the subject at hand or when we are paralyzed by roadblocks such as stress and low self-esteem?

In this section, we will seek to identify some common wealth-sabotaging attitudes and behaviors. I will then present strategies that I've successfully adopted to combat these roadblocks and to generally get out of my own way. The strategies that have worked for me may or may not work for you. They are presented for the purpose of getting you to think about what might work for you.

Are You a Money Magnet or a Wealth Repellant?

Disagreements over money issues are among the top causes of all breakups. They are also a leading cause of stress in nonromantic relationships. Before dealing with money problems and/or goals within a relationship, I believe we all need to periodically evaluate our solo financial lives. I always try to incorporate one or two financial goals into each SLC. It is hypocritical and counterproductive to comment on my partner's financial decisions without first ensuring that my own house is in order.

A healthy relationship with money is, in my opinion, more important than simply having a lot of money. Earning tons of money or being wealthy is often the result of happenstance. I can think of more than one megacelebrity whose stratospheric level of fame baffles me. *Really?* I think. *She can't even sing that well.* Others in the "accidentally wealthy" category include the children and grandchildren of business titans. Many of these folks do appear to be happy and glamorous, but the number of rehab stints, arrests, and messy divorces would suggest otherwise. Anyone who needs evidence that simply having more money is not necessarily a good thing need only look at the mind-blowing statistics of lottery winners. Well over half of all lottery winners lose every cent within two years of the big win. Two of my clients won lotteries only to lose everything within short order. One of them actually ended up declaring bankruptcy, which was a far worse financial position than he was in prior to the win. How could that possibly happen?

TOM'S STORY

Tom was the son of longtime clients of mine. He hit six out of six numbers on New York Lotto, and his after-tax haul on the lump sum payout was $975,000. He opted against the annuity, which could have provided him with a generous yearly payment for the rest of his life. His parents called to share the good news and ask if I had any legal advice for Tom. I recommended that he create an asset protection trust to hold at least one-half of the winnings. This would create a firewall to protect Tom against all of the lunatics, who I knew would soon descend. Tom agreed that it was a good idea and promised to make an appointment straightaway—upon his return from the Amalfi Coast.

The next thing I heard was that he had divorced his wife of eighteen years, and despite his initial vow to keep his job with UPS, he did, in fact, quit. He decided to invest what was left after the divorce and six months of pursuing wine, women, and song into a Johnny Rockets burger franchise. The business was very slow in taking off, and he did not anticipate having to front the large amounts of money necessary to keep it going during the first year. He had only focused on the best-case scenario presented during the franchise sales pitch. Tom proceeded to go through all of his winnings. He also borrowed against his UPS retirement plan and even hit his parents up for $20,000. Tom is now living with them in his childhood bedroom.

The only real winner was his ex-wife. She used the divorce settlement as a down payment on a two-family brownstone in Brooklyn. The rental income provides her with a net positive monthly cash flow. Tom never did make it in to see me about any estate planning. Now, he doesn't really need it . . . His parents, however, were recently in to revise their wills to reflect the $20,000 "loan" to Tom that they know they will never get back. His ultimate interest in their estate will thus be reduced.

It is easy to see all of the missteps that led to Tom losing the money. Less obvious, though, are the internal factors that were responsible for his poor decisions in the first place. The truth is that Tom never had a healthy relationship with money. The lottery win simply magnified his lack of discipline, poor financial knowledge, and failure to have any plan for his future. Tom grew up feeling like he never had all of the things that the other kids had. He dreamed of one day being able to have and do and spend whatever he wanted. Tom didn't grow up in poverty. His parents had stable jobs, and they had a comfortable, if not luxurious, existence. Tom never saw his parents fight over money. He never even really heard them talk about money at all. He knew that they lived within their means but wished that they would spend more on luxury items like he saw other families doing. As an adult, Tom didn't have any financial goals to speak of. He was more interested in acquiring things and taking nice vacations than he was in putting money away regularly for his retirement. He always thought that there would be plenty of time to save money later in life.

The problem is that true financial security doesn't just happen. Even a boatload of money can't provide financial security if one hasn't learned to master his or her relationship with money. If you are like me, you may not have received this education as a child. However, it is never too late to undertake a focused education and develop personal power over money. Do you wish to be in control of your financial future, or are you simply hoping for the best as you are confronted with a series of financial challenges?

One of the recurring items in my own SLC is something I call "financial boot camp." This is a one- or two-week period during which we, as a family, eliminate all possible discretionary spending. It is a challenge to see just how little we can actually spend. I don't buy clothing, shoes, or makeup during this time. We don't order any take-out food. It is the "now or never" zone for the mystery items in the deep freezer. In the morning, I pull something out of the freezer and let it defrost on the counter. I then put beans or a grain with vegetables and soup base into a crockpot. At the end of the day, the defrosted mystery dish is reheated, and voilà, dinner is served. Our weekend entertainment consists of free local concerts, park activities, bike rides, and board games. I don't even use disposable items like paper towels during financial-boot-camp weeks. Lest you fear receiving an invitation to visit, please know that I make an exception for toilet paper!

I feel like I need to go through this process periodically to strengthen my power over money. It is sort of like the financial

equivalent of a juice cleanse. Having had a financially chaotic childhood, I was a disaster with money as a young adult. I couldn't rest
if there was some open space on one of my credit cards. It took me
several years to climb out of this mess. I am now in what anyone
would consider a very strong financial position. However, I do notice
that when my guard is down, bad spending habits tend to reemerge.
Convenience expenditures such as take-out food for dinner escalate;
I buy yet another oatmeal-colored sweater; I buy yet more math
workbooks that my kids will successfully fight against using. The list
goes on and on. By periodically *stopping* all nonessential spending, I
feel that I am reclaiming my power over money. During a financial-
boot-camp week, I try to reread one of the great books that help me
to gain mastery over my inner spendthrift ways. These include works
by Benjamin Franklin, Suze Orman, Dave Ramsey, Robert Kiyosaki,
Jack Canfield, and the Beardstown Ladies.

I consider myself to be a student of money behavior, and I am
always intrigued by my clients who don't necessarily earn that much
every year still but manage to build very impressive nest eggs. Conversely, I have seen more than a few high-living big earners who have
difficulty swinging their country-club dues and many other obligations each month. Sometimes, their blue-collar parents, with their
out-of-date, avocado-green kitchen appliances and rotary phones are
called upon to make "loans" to their well-dressed and high-living
children.

A few years back, I formed a group that I called Money Magnets Savings Club. This was a group of women who got together in
my office conference room one evening each week. We took turns
bringing (homemade) dinner in. The agenda consisted of sharing
advice gleaned from various personal finance readings. We would
have a guest speaker who educated us on specific financial topics.
We would trade all sorts of money-saving tips with one another.
We brainstormed on methods for each of us to not only cut back
on expenditures but also generate additional revenue. A few of the
members launched businesses that were a direct result of our group
experience. Each meeting began by having us take turns recounting
the prior week's financial victories and challenges. What nonessential spending were we able to reduce or eliminate? What slipups or

setbacks did we experience? Did we cave in to the pleading and nagging of the fifteen-year-old who wanted $120 sneakers?

I have come to truly believe the old adage that by spending less than we are able to, we can powerfully ensure that we will always have more than we need. Yes, I can and do admire my friends' Hermes Birkin bags. However, I could never justify a $10,000-plus pocket book regardless of whether I can afford to buy it or not. I smile imagining my smart-aleck former Money Magnets members telling me that the Birkin bag won't make my rear end look any slimmer. The extra $10,000 in my 401K, however, does make me sleep better at night.

Having authentic conversations about money was a new experience for many of us in the group. It is often easier to talk to friends about everything else in the world. We are more likely to be open and honest about sexual issues, relationship problems, and workplace challenges than we are about household budgeting. I'm not sure why we are so reluctant to talk about money, but the process is empowering.

I learned several things from the Money Magnets experience, the most important of which is that it is essential to surround oneself with people who offer support and encouragement. Any goal is more easily reached if I am in the company of "fellow travelers" dealing with their own successes and setbacks. We all know that it is sometimes easier to objectively assess and give constructive input to the problems of others than it is to diagnose and work on our own problems. What I learned with Money Magnets, though, is that the act of offering support, encouragement, and sound advice to another person in a situation similar to our own has the effect of powerfully imparting this guidance into our own psyches. I found myself more easily able to say no to a relative who wanted yet another "loan," because I felt the strength of my group and could imagine them shaking their heads in shared frustration with me if I were to tell them that I had to deal with this again.

The Money Magnets experience confirmed for me what I had observed working with thousands of clients on their estate planning. One's ability to generate and retain wealth bears a strong relationship to certain internal traits. People whose wealth is more than accidental and temporary share a few undeniable characteristics: they don't live above their means; they constantly seek to acquire new information; they have personal vitality; they live in surroundings that please them; and they don't allow themselves to be hobbled by personal roadblocks. These observations form the bases of goals that I include in each SLC that I create.

Constant Pursuit of Knowledge

Knowledge is universally understood to be an essential element of power. We could all stand to engage in periodic introspection in order to increase our self-knowledge, and we should also be constantly striving to acquire new external information. I am often mystified to see so many clients and acquaintances who enter into business transactions without sufficient knowledge to evaluate the deal and all of its possible ramifications. Collaborating and contracting without adequate knowledge will almost certainly leave us holding the short end of the stick.

Lack of knowledge can sometimes be attributed to willful ignorance. In this category, I think of all of the Ponzi-scheme victims. They were so thrilled to see the doctored statements showing double-digit investment returns that they didn't really want to investigate any further. Of course, they knew, logically, that they shouldn't invest all of their assets with one person or company. Yet, willful ignorance kept them stuck and resulted in devastating losses for thousands.

Acquiring knowledge is, in my opinion, the most important starting point to identifying and addressing internal deficiencies as well as maximizing the success of one's collaborations and negotiations with others. As it relates to legal transactions, how does one best acquire the legal knowledge necessary to understand and evaluate a given transaction? You could go to law school—though this probably isn't the most efficient way. The correct answer, of course, is to hire a lawyer. But how in the world can you be sure that the attorney you select actually has the knowledge and motivation to protect you?

As a practicing attorney, I want my clients to have as much information as possible about the legal transactions we engage in. When someone says to me that they have no desire to truly understand the details of what we are doing, because they trust me, I promptly put the brakes on the proceeding. I don't want my clients to ever feel that they jumped into something that they were not familiar with. Instead, I urge the people I work with to push against their comfort zones in order to fully understand what I am trying to accomplish for them. The more my clients know, the better the results are. This is because they are transformed from a passive bystander waiting to be told where to sign into an active partner. Together, my client and I can sculpt a truly customized solution to whatever problem presents itself.

Shouldn't you be able to trust that your lawyer knows what she is doing? Ideally, yes, but in reality, your attorney may not be acting in your best interests. She may be having a bad day, or she may not, in fact, actually know what she is doing. This point was hammered home for me several years back.

There is an attorney with whom I was "socially friendly." I would see "Fred" at Bar Association functions and community events. Fred was an established personal injury attorney and had what I thought was a flourishing practice.

One day, Fred called to ask if I would review a trust that he was preparing for a client. I thought it was very strange that Fred was doing a trust, because I knew him to be a personal injury attorney. In any event, I agreed to look at it. He faxed it to my office, and I took it home that weekend. From my couch perch, pen in hand, I proceeded to go through the document.

As an aside, I must tell you that as a trusts and estates attorney, I do everything possible to stay current with changing laws and tax-code provisions. My husband often refers to me as a geek in this regard. Can one ever be too diligent, though, when it comes to ensuring that a client's nest egg or home is optimally protected? It is with this mindset that I examined Fred's trust.

It was the legal document equivalent of a horror movie. This trust referred to provisions of the US tax code that had been repealed decades earlier! It was a total piece of garbage, and it was immediately clear to me where Fred had gotten the template. He must have somehow inherited the files of some retired or deceased old-time attorney. He then must have had his secretary cut and paste his client's name and information into the document. It was a disaster, and I wasn't sure what I should do. It would have been very awkward for me to candidly share my thoughts with Fred. On the other hand, I didn't want his client to be hurt by this bad trust. I decided to call Fred on Monday and learn more about his client's situation. I then created a trust that I believed would meet these objectives. Fred thanked me for the trust and then proceeded to hang a shingle outside of his office announcing his new trusts and estates practice! Little did he know that the particular trust I gave him was only one of many dozens that I used. I imagined that all of his unsuspecting trusts and estates clients left his office with that particular trust. There was at least a statistical chance that it was the right trust for their situation—that is, until I stopped using it because of a change in law.

I do hope that Fred will make the effort to learn something about this new area of law that he has entered into. If he chooses to remain ignorant, though, this will definitely cost his clients in terms of unprotected assets. Eventually, the ignorance will also cost Fred, by way of a barrage of inevitable lawsuits.

Should Fred's clients also have some responsibility for possibly putting themselves in a bad situation? Just because an attorney might look the part and sound the part does not necessarily mean that he is optimally prepared to protect you, your family, and your wealth. How on earth, though, can you determine whether an attorney is competent prior to engaging him? Online reviews can be misleading in that positive ones can be "planted" and negative ones can be posted by a beneficiary who is unhappy with what he or she received in an estate. The reviewer may, therefore, be angry with the attorney, even though he didn't do anything wrong.

I encourage people to have phone conversations with a few attorneys before scheduling an initial consultation. You can get an idea as to whether you and they will be compatible. This is an important and potentially long-term relationship you are embarking on. You need to be willing to trust this person with secrets that you might not even share with your closest friends. Liking them just a little will make this process easier.

Once you have a few agreeable candidates, how do you determine whether or not they know what they are talking about? How can you test an attorney's knowledge without being an attorney yourself? There are several methods. Some attorneys hold community presentations at libraries or local colleges. This is a good environment in which to ask questions and judge for yourself whether the explanation makes sense. I would think twice about engaging an attorney who tried to impress me with his or her brilliance. Yes, we all learned extraordinary words and impressive Latin phrases in law school. Unfortunately, some of these must be included in legal documents for them to successfully accomplish your goals. However, someone who truly understands what they are talking about should have no trouble explaining concepts clearly and plainly to someone who happens to be in another profession.

Once you have selected your attorney and created a trust and other legal documents to protect your wealth, your education process still isn't done. It is essential to stay informed about current laws and meet with your attorney periodically to give her new information about your personal situation. Remember that the legal documents that may have perfectly protected you one year ago definitely need to be updated if your husband develops dementia or another beneficiary has a new problem.

By committing to the continued acquisition and exchange of legal information, you are doing everything within your power to avoid and prevent the loss of wealth.

Committing to the continuous acquisition of knowledge can also enable us to strengthen our internal wealth-building capacities. I believe that the lifelong pursuit of self-improvement elevates one's overall sense of well-being. As a "human work in progress," I never stop acquiring new knowledge and trying to improve every aspect of my life. I learn the best ways to deal with life's inevitable setbacks and disappointments. I refuse to let these setbacks sideline me and sap me of the personal power that keeps me moving forward. Commitment to expanded knowledge and forward momentum can also make us more effective and productive in our careers, business dealings, wealth acquisition, and interpersonal relationships.

Commitment to Physical Vitality

Optimal nutrition and exercise are essential components to the development and strengthening of one's vitality and personal power. Increased physical vitality will allow us to have more working and wealth-building years, thereby resulting in a bigger nest egg. Commitment to continuous improvement in one's nutrition and exercise cannot help but put us on the road to enhanced vitality and personal power, which, in turn, can help us to attract wealth and repel wealth destroyers.

NUTRITION

It is impossible to have optimal physical vitality if we are constantly putting the wrong fuel into our bodies. Yes, we all already know that the nightly bag of chips in front of the TV isn't doing us any favors. Most people I know have had periodic bouts of bad nutritional habits. If you have tried unsuccessfully to adopt healthier eating habits, then resolve to at least learn more about healthful eating. The smallest positive movement is the first one on the path forward. Never allow setbacks to derail you, because diet and nutrition are always a work in progress. I happen to have many overweight people in my family. Because of this, I have usually tried to be mindful about what I eat. College was definitely an exception to this. During these years, offerings from vending machines and the mall food court made up way too big a percentage of my daily food intake. Then there was law school, when my diet bore a strong resemblance to that of a teenage runaway. I now always endeavor to keep up with the latest (admittedly often conflicting) information on nutrition. I am also on the constant lookout for clues about what works best for me. I know that certain foods can increase health and vitality and other foods can diminish it. I also know that there are several foods I cannot resist. Using this knowledge about nutrition and my own weaknesses in this regard, I try to live by a few rules that work for me. One of my personal rules is to not have certain things in the house that I am powerless to resist. The "everything in moderation" mantra may work for some people, but it definitely would not work to prevent me from eating as many peanut butter cups as I can lay my hands on.

Always on the lookout for the latest nutrition intel, I sift through a wide array of information and decide what guidance resonates with me and what doesn't. At the end of the day, any method of improving the quality of the food we eat and reducing the overall number of calories consumed will probably point us in the right direction. Whether I accomplish this by going vegan, vegetarian, wheat-free, gluten-free, dairy-free, low carb, low fat, paleo, or raw food, learning what can work in my life is the single most important piece of nutritional knowledge I can acquire. When I try something and it works for me, then I incorporate that information into my SLC.

One of the most recent nutritional additions to my SLC was picked up in Tim Ferris's book *The 4-Hour Workweek*. For the few of you who haven't read this gem, I strongly recommend it. The primary focus of the book is on reinventing one's career to dramatically improve efficiency. The resulting free time allows the successful reader to pursue adventure, joy, and passion. In the book, Mr. Ferris describes employing the "80/20" rule to several areas of one's life, including nutrition. He advocates adhering to disciplined food consumption 80 percent of the time and letting 'er rip during the remaining 20 percent of the time. The first chapter opens with a vivid depiction of Mr. Ferris consuming way too many donuts because it is his dedicated "free day." While I do need to reread the book to get closer to a four-hour workweek, I was instantaneously able to understand and incorporate the "one-day free" nutritional philosophy. It thus made its way into my SLC.

I do eat whatever I want on both weekend days. I have probably taken the weekends-off philosophy a bit too far. Would it be better if I ate lean fish, whole grains, and plenty of fruits and vegetables every single day? Absolutely. Am I able to successfully do this, at this particular period of my life? Absolutely not. I wouldn't even set myself up for failure by trying. Instead, I do the very best I can during the week. My weeknight dinners often consist of steamed broccoli, a

veggie burger, and a baked sweet potato. Sunday nights, however, are
reserved for a little tradition I like to call "Piglet Fest." I can be found
on the couch, in front of the TV, with bags of chips and all sorts of
assorted snacks laid out around me. The treats are washed down, of
course, with my favorite chardonnay. On Monday morning, I feel
rather like a tick ready to pop on account of my crazy sodium intake.

When deciding what nutritional goals should be included in each
version of my SLC, I employ a modified version of the contract process. This tool increases my chances of sticking with the goals, because
it keeps out things that are highly unlikely to work for me. Applying
the contract process to my own nutritional life works like this:

1. *Q: What do I want?* A: I want to increase the percentage of
   fruits and vegetables in my diet and reduce fatty, processed,
   and sodium-laden foods.
2. *Q: What am I able and willing to do to accomplish this goal?*
   Am I able and willing to give up my Sunday evening Piglet Fest?
   A: NO.
3. *Q: Is there any maneuverability?* A: Perhaps I can stop eating
   an hour earlier on Sunday nights. This will give my body an
   extra hour to metabolize everything before going to bed. I
   am willing to do this, so I incorporate it into my solo love
   contract. Perhaps I can also adopt the practice of going for
   a walk before going to bed now that I have the extra time.
   This sounds like a great idea, but I know myself well enough
   to know that it is unrealistic. The *last* thing that I feel like
   doing after I throw out my empty chip bags and put the
   empty chardonnay bottle in the recycling bin is anything else
   that requires movement. This idea will not make its way into
   my SLC at this time. Can I reduce the frequency of Piglet
   Fest to every other Sunday? Hmm, this is a tough call. After
   careful consideration, though, I reject the idea. However, I
   am open to considering it the next time I review and tweak
   this contract. Am I willing to reduce my total sodium intake
   by substituting air-popped popcorn for one of my three bags
   of chips? Yes, I am willing to do this, so it will become part
   of my solo love contract. I am also committed to continuing

to improve my knowledge about nutrition. In each of my SLCs, I include rereading *The 20/20 Diet*. I have successfully utilized the five-day Phase I of this book any time I need a nutritional "course correction" and some quick motivation.

EXERCISE

Together with nutrition, our level of physical fitness contributes directly to our overall physical vitality and energy levels. As an estate planning and elder law attorney, I spend a lot of time, each day, with people in their eighties and nineties. Sometimes, I am truly shocked when some of my clients share their dates of birth—it doesn't seem possible because they look so great! I never fail to ask them for life advice that I can incorporate into my next SLC. I can tell you that one of the central themes in all of their answers has to do with movement. They tell me that they just keep moving every day.

I recently gave up the manhunt for the criminal who stole my waist. I have accepted the harsh reality that we need to increase the amount we exercise each year to combat the effects of slowing metabolisms. This is why I always try to implement a few new exercise goals every time I create a new SLC.

Again, applying the contracting process to my SLC goal selection increases my chances of sticking with the goals, because they have gone through a structured and rigorous vetting. Last year, for example, I considered adopting the goal of running a marathon in my SLC. I ended up deciding against it. It was a close call, though. Because it was so close, I decided to table the goal for possible inclusion in this year's SLC. Applying the three-step contracting process causes me to ask:

1. *Q: Do I wish to run a marathon?* A: Yes! It would be great to be part of what looks like such a party atmosphere. I can imagine my husband and children holding up cardboard signs reading, "Way to go, Ann!" I am smiling just thinking about that awesome day.
2. *Q: What am I willing to do to reach the goal of being able to complete a marathon? Am I willing to devote twenty or more*

hours per week for several months training for the race? A. Yes, I am willing. However, I am not able to accommodate the time commitment given my current scheduling demands.

3. *Q: Is there any leeway or maneuverability? Can I find a way to make it work?* A: Well, I could wake up at three o'clock in the morning to get in a few running hours before I have to start getting the kids ready for school. People I know and respect do this. I can't quite imagine that this would be realistic for me, though. When I think of the predawn hours on a twenty-degree February morning, there is only one place I want to be, and sneakers don't belong there. The bottom line is that running a marathon will, again, be tabled. For me, the contract process had the effect of objectifying this decision. I'm not deciding against the marathon because I am a lazy loser. Rather, I gave it due consideration and believe that I am perfectly willing and able to commit to this goal. It simply doesn't comfortably fit into my life at this juncture.

Whenever I learn about a new exercise finding, I consider incorporating it into my SLC. A few months ago, I learned about the plank exercise. This is where your feet and hands are on the floor and your back is as straight as possible. It is the beginning position for a push up. Instead of lowering into a push up, however, the plank requires us to hold the pose for as long as we can. This is *much* harder than it may seem. The plank made it onto my SLC where the marathon did not, because I can control the time spent on this exercise. It can, therefore, be made to fit into my current daily life. It turns out that it is a challenge for me to hold the plank for two minutes. So, I resolved to do the plank three times a day. Six minutes per day results in an additional three hours per month of isometric work on my core. Compared to three class hours of exercise with required travel time and preparation, the plank saves me time as well as money!

What on earth does fitness have to do with building and keeping wealth? I have observed a high level of correlation between one's fitness and wealth levels.

HEATHER'S STORY

Consider Heather. She could probably stand to lose ten pounds but is not what anyone would call overweight. She is, however, dreadfully unfit with terrible eating and lifestyle habits. She is thirty-two years old and works as an account executive for a medical malpractice insurer. With Heather's low energy levels, it is a chore to drag herself to work and then crawl home every night. Sapped of vitality as a result of poor food choices and lack of exercise, she is kept stuck in this rut. Headed home from work, she cannot begin to imagine summoning the energy to cook dinner. So what does she do? She brings home yet more take-out food and eats it in front of the TV.

She jokes to friends that the only vegetables she consumes are in the form of pizza toppings. Fruit? There must be some in her favorite strawberry ice cream. Does she feel like taking a walk or doing some other type of exercise after dinner (and a drink or two or three)? No way. She is usually even too tired to get up from the couch and go to bed at a reasonable hour. Heather then watches more TV than she planned and goes to bed later than she planned. This leaves her barely able to drag herself out of bed in the morning—and the whole saga repeats itself.

Determined to turn things around, Heather joined a gym, but she never goes. At work, she is well liked, but her performance, in terms of getting doctors to sign up for the company's malpractice coverage, is rather pathetic. She hasn't received a raise in three years and believes that her job security is not great. Heather knows that she should be saving money in preparation for the very real possibility that she will be fired. Unfortunately, and despite the fact that she hardly ever goes out socializing and never buys new clothes,

she hasn't been able to save anything in the five years
she's been at the company. Let's look at the numbers:

    Heather's salary: $42,000
    Commissions for each new doctor signed up: $0
    Heather's monthly after-tax income: $2,625
    Rent, utilities, and transportation costs: $1,600
    Groceries: $300
    Takeout food: $450
    Gym membership: $60
    Premium cable TV package: $100

This leaves Heather with approximately $115 for clothing,
entertainment, and savings. Is Heather a money magnet?
No way! With every bite of her overprocessed and sodium-laden diet, she powerfully pushes her existing money
as well as wealth-building potential out of her grasp.

Being overweight or unfit can cause us to spend
whatever wealth we have managed to accumulate. Trying
to lose weight is very expensive. It is estimated that
the US weight-loss industry makes $60 billion per year
from people willing to try repeatedly to get a handle
on their physical state. In Heather's case, her unused
gym membership costs her $720 per year. According to
Statisticbrain.com, 67 percent of Americans with gym
memberships never use them. Factor in her diet sodas,
weight-loss books, and the various exercise machines
she purchased over the years, and it is easy to see how
the costs of unsuccessful fitness attempts can add up.

Everyone, including Heather, knows that she needs
to make some changes. It is a classic catch-22, though.
Heather's lack of energy has long prevented her from making the life changes necessary to increase her energy.

Heather did, eventually, manage to turn things
around. How? She didn't do it on her own, and she

didn't throw more money at the problem. She asked for advice from her coworker, Beth, who, at fifty-seven, is the poster child of health and vitality. Beth was flattered and moved by the overture and thus committed to sharing a few pages from her playbook.

Several years earlier, Beth went through a painful and financially devastating divorce. She was determined to turn things around for herself, both in terms of her finances and her health. She shared the story with Heather about the Sunday morning she started. That magical first day of the rest of her life began by sleeping in. Beth wanted to be well rested. She began the day with a three-mile walk around her neighborhood. She then went to the supermarket and used her smartphone to find a recipe that employed the two cheapest vegetables there. She bought five food storage containers, a bag of Garbonzo beans, and uncooked popcorn kernels. Beth's new healthy habits were propelled by the actions of that first day. She prepared a healthy plant-based dinner and stored two extra portions in the fridge and three in the freezer. She vowed to drastically reduce take-out foods and relied on fruit, air-popped popcorn, and a refrigerated bowl of cooked beans for snacks.

Heather was inspired to turbocharge her own physical vitality. Her power walk on that first day yielded immediate financial rewards. Usually too lazy and tired to organize her refrigerator, Heather set about making a big chopped salad with what could be salvaged from her vegetable bin. Fruit that wouldn't last much longer was cut up and frozen for weekday breakfast smoothies. Throwing out expired containers enabled her to accurately assess what remained, thereby avoiding duplicate purchases. On Beth's advice, she stopped short of vowing to end all takeout. Such blanket declarations can set us up for failure with the inevitable deviation. Instead,

like Beth, she vowed to dramatically reduce takeout.
She didn't follow a specific nutrition plan but simply
opted for more plant-based foods and less fat, sugar,
and salt. She eliminated diet sodas and bought a water
filtration attachment for her kitchen faucet. She quit
her gym membership and developed her own thirty-minute
routine. This consisted of doing five minutes of jog-
ging, marching, jumping jacks, push-ups, sit-ups, and
squats while watching TV after dinner. Weather permit-
ting, Heather now also goes for a fifteen- to twenty-
minute walk before her breakfast smoothie.

How do these lifestyle changes improve Heather's
financial bottom line? She eliminated her premium
cable TV package. She quit her gym membership and lowered her monthly take-out food bill by $400 while only
increasing her supermarket bill by $200. Her income
has also picked up in the form of commissions. Heather
now has the physical stamina and confidence to go out
on sales calls to physicians and has succeeded in
getting a number of them to sign on to her company's
malpractice insurance. Her new monthly budget looks
like this:

Heather's salary: $42,000
Commissions for new doctors signed up this month: $500
Heather's monthly after-tax monthly income: $3,000
Rent, utilities, and transportation costs: $1,600
Groceries: $500
Take out food: $50
Gym membership: $0
Basic cable TV package: $50

This leaves Heather with an extra $800 per month with
which to save, invest, and donate to her favorite
charities.

There are certainly things in life that are beyond our control: height, childhood circumstances, and early education are a few. Diet and exercise, however? That is easy! Forward progress is a process rather than a destination. As such, I can begin the process right now by drinking eight ounces of water and doing the plank for two minutes. In less than five minutes, I have hydrated my cells and strengthened my muscles. This is a no-fail technique to feeling greater vitality and tends to lead to better food choices at my next meal.

SURROUNDINGS

What do physical surroundings have to do with one's financial bottom line? As should be apparent by now, I believe that every single aspect of our lives affects our financial bottom line. Our finances, in turn, impact every other area of life. I have seen, time and again, how personal power can be optimized by the right physical surroundings. Our home environment is truly the stage on which our lives play out. A beautiful, serene, and orderly environment sends a powerful message to our subconscious that we are basically in control of our life's many moving parts. A messy, disorganized, or dirty environment, on the other hand, sends the message that things have gotten beyond our control. We have, by the looks of it, signaled surrender to one or more challenges in our daily lives. This is a circular proposition. The more powerful and in control I feel, the better able I am to wrestle my surroundings into submission. This, like our other personal power components, is always a work in progress. There is always room to enhance our surroundings—no matter how great or how disorderly they happen to be right now.

Partners often have different levels of organizational skills and requirements. This is a pretty common source of conflict—within my own house as well as for the couples I work with. Before working on this issue with a partner, however, it is vitally important to exert control and effect positive change over those aspects of our physical surroundings that we are able to.

In keeping with our goal of not spending money unnecessarily, it is important to point out that having beautiful and serene surroundings has absolutely nothing to do with money. I know this for a fact after having visited hundreds of clients' homes over the years. I have one megawealthy client who I don't think ever fully unloads her dishwasher. Instead, she only takes out what is needed for a meal, puts the items back in when dirty, runs the cycle, and repeats this at the next meal. I believe there are things that have not come out of that dishwasher since the George H. W. Bush administration. I am sure that a psychologist would be able to offer up some possible diagnoses for this behavior. My role is more limited. I offer possible remedies to the behavior. The way to deal with the effects is pretty simple: *make a decision.*

I view almost all clutter and disorganization as a direct consequence of one's inability to make an immediate decision. Catalogs that come in the mail, broken household objects, outgrown clothes, kids toys, goodie bag trinkets, solo socks—the list is truly endless. It is very easy to put any given object to the side with the intention of deciding what best to do with it later. The problem with this procrastination, though, is that in the modern world, we are rarely blessed with free days during which we can deal with all of these decisions. There is, unfortunately, no magical day during which it would be preferable to engage in many hours of hard-core organizing rather than spend our limited free time with friends and family. The results of our ambivalence are spore-like piles of stuff all over the place. Most of us have junk drawers with old keys, takeout menus, hardware, and dried-out glue containers. Without constant vigilance, the "sickness" in this drawer spreads and threatens to take over territory on the kitchen counter, the dining room table, and dresser tops.

In the context of creating a love contract, I find it impossible to effectively dialogue with a partner about how he might improve in this area without first "walking the walk" myself. We want to avoid a negative spiral caused by thoughts such as "What does it matter whether I am vigilant about busting through masses of clutter if my partner is Messy Marvin?" We need to remember that the solo organization section of the SLC is preparatory to dealing with the issue with my partner in our joint love contract.

In my life, I commit to making immediate decisions on every new piece of matter that enters my personal domain. My serene and peaceful surroundings are so important to me that I view every new item with suspicion. It must "earn" its place in my home. In the case of a new piece of clothing, I make sure to eliminate the exact number of pieces of existing clothing that are coming in the door. The lost sock? It gets a stay of execution for exactly four weeks to see if its mate is belatedly spat out of the laundry room bowels. If not, into the big black garbage bag it goes.

I love big black garbage bags. Whenever I have a spare half hour, I bring two into any given room. I scan every item in the room and make instantaneous decisions. Does it stay? Do I put it in the garbage black bag? Or do I put it in the charity black bag? For tax-deduction purposes, it is a good idea to keep a series of file folders each year. One of mine is marked "clothing." I put every new clothing receipt into this file. A few years down the road when an item is being donated, I have the receipt to establish the original value. No, I can't deduct the full price five years later, but it is a helpful starting point from which to arrive upon a reasonable value. The garbage bag forays are best conducted outside of the presence of one's partner or children. I have found that we all have very different ideas about what items are essential.

Having organized surroundings is an essential element of having mastery over one's life. It also helps boost feelings of strength and power in our dealings and negotiations with others. In the workplace, our physical surroundings can affect our mood and outlook. It can also send powerful messages to our colleagues, supervisors, and clients. Lawyers are notorious for working amid massive mountains of clutter. I wonder, though, what prospective clients would think if they saw huge stacks of other clients' files in disorganized piles all over my desk and floor. They would probably be correct in thinking that I am barely keeping up with my existing caseload and am already stretched too thin. They would most likely not be very eager to retain my services. Relatedly, I believe that a cluttered work environment reduces one's promotion prospects. I said earlier that you don't need money to become organized. However, being very organized can powerfully maximize one's wealth prospects. The visual signal to my supervisors and clients is that I am more than capable of taking on more work and responsibility.

In maintaining my organized office and home, I confess to having a secret helper. Martha Stewart is kind enough to make time to visit my home and office and regularly offers helpful tips to me—in my imagination anyway. Try looking at your surroundings through the eyes of someone you imagine possesses the penultimate levels of orderliness and taste. This cannot help but result in new ideas.

In my SLC, organizational items include committing to the two-bag exercise at least twice a month as well as a weekly visit and critique from Martha Stewart.

Takeaways

1. Commit to constant self-improvement and an ever-expanding knowledge base.
2. Getting a handle on nutrition and physical fitness will turbocharge your personal power. There is no single formula to accomplish this. Use personal experimentation and the contract process to implement winning strategies for yourself.
3. Commit to transforming your home and work surroundings into beautiful and organized spaces. This will boost feelings of mastery over one's life and will also expand one's wealth-building potential.

11

ELIMINATING PERSONAL ROADBLOCKS TO WEALTH

After adopting a few SLC provisions to boost our nutrition, exercise, and physical surroundings, it is time to consider how fear, low self-esteem, and stress can prevent forward progress and hurt our relationships, negotiations, and overall wealth-building potential. By implementing just a few strategies, we can eliminate these stubborn roadblocks to optimal prosperity and rewarding relationships.

Fear

I ask my clients to consider how fear may be preventing them from reaching their full potential as individuals and as couples. My unscientific conclusion, based on my work with thousands of clients, is that fear of embarrassment is the number one obstacle that stands in the way of reaching one's full potential. We may think and say that we want to live boldly and courageously but find it easier to remain in a sort of holding pattern within our comfort zones.

I encourage everyone to include one or two fear busters in their SLCs. These action items may be physical challenges such as zip-lining or skiing or things like flying in a plane or driving over a bridge. If you want to start at the top, studies show that the number one fear is public speaking. People are often paralyzed with fear at the prospect of having to give a best man or maid of honor toast at a wedding. Though it can produce some wildly entertaining results, doing shots before the toast is probably not the best strategy to overcome this fear. I have more than one friend who confessed to not serving as a maid of honor only because she couldn't imagine giving the speech. I believe this fear directly limits one's earning potential and by extension his or her wealth. Fear of public speaking prevents the real estate agent, financial advisor, accountant, or salesperson from holding seminars at the local library or community group, which could double his or her business with no advertising costs. Anyone who is serious about eliminating wealth sabotagers needs to vanquish the fear of public speaking.

How can we successfully get over a deep-seated fear such as public speaking?

Yes, you know the answer: *just do it*. What's the worst that can happen? Will people laugh at me? Will I make a complete fool out of myself? Quite possibly—but that isn't always such a bad thing.

When I decided to run for the NYS legislature the year after graduating from law school, I had never made a speech or even given a toast in my entire life. I knew that running for the position would require more than a few speeches. So would the job itself if I somehow managed to win the election. I was frightened out of my mind at the prospect of public speaking but gamely assured myself that it wouldn't be that bad.

My early speeches can be described as nothing short of cringeworthy. With no staff to help me and no time to do much research, I was never quite sure of what to mention or who to thank at each of the several dozen civic and community groups I addressed. More often than not, I misspoke and managed to offend people wherever I went.

My biggest public-speaking embarrassment came several months after I managed to win that first election. Within weeks of being sworn in, I began to feel much more comfortable speaking in front of groups of all sizes. I even began to think that I might have some natural public-speaking talent. With a staff to assist me now, I could rely on people to research issues of importance to the many groups I appeared before each week. My staff would give me separate manila envelopes that held the information I needed for each presentation. When time permitted, I would study the information in advance, but more often than not, I only had a few minutes in my car to look everything over, memorize a few nuggets, and then go in and wow them! I was pretty darn sure of myself at this point. That is, until the Yeats celebration . . . This event was going to be a big one for me. It was to be held at the Yeats Tavern in Bayside. Not impressive sounding, I know, but it was going to be televised locally as well as live—in Ireland! I fantasized that this would be the first small step toward my dream job of becoming an ambassador. Yes—Ambassador Ann Margaret!

Weeks before the event, I asked my staff to pull together a lot of background information on Yeats. I kept the fat manila envelope in the file box in my car that held my weekly schedule and materials for each group I was to address. Because this event was so important to me, I planned to study for it in advance. Alas, this did not come to pass. No bother, I had a solid twenty minutes prior to my speaking time to read up. I parked the car and pulled out the envelope, prepared to read, memorize, then go in and dazzle! I proceeded to open the envelope and found five articles on Billy Yates the Ozark Yodeler! What!? My staff later told me that I never specified which Yeats I needed research on . . . (You try firing a civil servant!)

This was way back in time when mobile phones had no information retrieval capabilities. They only made calls. For the next five minutes, mine only reached voicemail. I tried to rack my brain for anything I might remember about Yeats from AP English in high school. Nothing. Then, I thought the event sponsors must surely have fliers with background information that I could grab and read in the ladies' room. Nope. I scoured the walls for a framed poem I could memorize and recite—anything. I was desperate. As a last resort, I asked the bartender if he could tell me anything about Yeats. He had a good laugh and said he was really looking forward to my keynote speech. OMG, I felt nauseated. I thought about bolting toward a door. Instead, I downed two shots of Jameson's, sat through the Irish and US national anthems, and braced for my name to be called. I never received such great applause as when I was introduced. Then came my first halting sentence: "What can be said about Yeats that hasn't been said before?" It went downhill from there. You could have heard a pin drop when I finished and slunk out the nearest exit.

I am living proof that no one has ever died from embarrassment. Quite the opposite. Today, I wouldn't trade that experience for anything. Not only does it never fail to give me a laugh, I do feel stronger for having gone through it. I no longer fear embarrassment, because I withstood it in its purest form. I feel inoculated against its limiting effects. Triumphing over the fear of being embarrassed has left me with a special type of armor that continues to serve me well many years later.

I heartily recommend running for elected office, if only for the countless opportunities to develop resistance to the fear of embarrassment. It is impossible to otherwise replicate the salutary effects of having had doors slammed in my face and insults hurled at me at polling sites and in debates. Asking family and friends for campaign money also provided unique opportunities for personal growth.

Once I announced by initial candidacy, I quickly learned that a competitive campaign was going to be an expensive proposition. Having recently graduated law school, I was still up to my eyeballs in student loan and credit card debt. How on earth could people know what it was that I wanted to do for them if I couldn't place newspaper ads or send direct mail? The answer, of course, was to throw a lot of fundraisers. There were only two problems with this: I didn't know anyone with money, and the campaign donors who did have money didn't know me. If I could only get a celebrity to cohost a fundraiser, then thousands of people would surely line up to contribute.

I remembered that a friend was related by marriage to the late Governor Mario Cuomo. Would he possibly be willing to lend his name to my fundraiser? "Consider it done," my friend answered. Great! I borrowed money from my uncle to have beautiful invitations printed. Another friend of a friend agreed to loan me her country estate for the high-profile event. We arranged for high school students to play the violin. The invitations went out and everything was in place. That was, until my friend called to let me know that Governor Cuomo was not on board with the fundraiser using his name. So much for "consider it done."

I didn't know what I was going to tell the hundreds of people coming to the fundraiser. Maybe the governor would surprise me by changing his mind and would show up after all. The surprise that I got instead was that no one at all showed up to the fundraiser. To this day, I'm not sure what happened. One hour after the appointed start time, it was clear to me that this was an unqualified disaster. The only silver lining was that there was no one to be embarrassed in front of—that is, until the lone car pulled into the driveway and a law school classmate exited, dressed in his best suit, ready to hobnob with bigwigs. Now, I thought that I would surely die of embarrassment. He reluctantly handed me his $100 check, wished me luck, and promptly left. Now I was only $400 in the hole on this event. This, too, was an experience that I am glad to have survived. Governor Cuomo ended up contributing to my campaign and had a laugh with me when I shared the story a few years later.

I encourage everyone to include one potentially embarrassing action item on your SLC. People who have overcome their fear of making fools of themselves can crack silly jokes, can sing off key in mixed company, and are generally a lot of fun to be around. In business, they aren't afraid to speak up and share their unconventional thoughts about doing things differently. They are liberated to give voice to innovative ideas. They are also far more likely to rise to leadership positions within an organization or start their own companies. If you are willing to take a polar-bear-type plunge into the icy waters of embarrassment, your career potential and long-term wealth prospects will be better off for it. Karaoke anyone?

Self-Esteem

It isn't possible to accomplish big goals or have positive dealings with others if we suffer from a negative self-image. Feelings of being "less than" can keep us from believing we have a chance to pursue the career or relationship we want. Lack of self-worth can keep us mired in dead-end jobs and relationships that don't serve us well. Lack of self-esteem can also hold us back from questioning any given agreement or proposed deal.

One easy exercise to improving self-esteem is to write down three or four of what you perceive to be your greatest shortcomings. Do you feel held back by a lack of education or a dislike of your physical appearance (too short, too tall, etc.)? Was your childhood a horror show? Do you have no savings? Next, imagine the type of life you would be living if you didn't suffer from these hardships? What kind of business would you be in? What types of relationships would you have? Now turn back to your list of negatives and come up with two or three celebrities or successful business people who share these supposedly negative characteristics. Of course, these "negatives" didn't hold them back. By all outward appearances, Danny DeVito doesn't seem to notice that there are actors who are taller than he is. He doesn't appear to give any energy to lamenting his lack of stature. Because he doesn't focus on this, neither do we.

As I entered my forties, I began to wonder whether this "was all she wrote" in terms of pursuing and reaching various financial and other life goals. In an effort to prevent my self-esteem from being hurt by my encroaching "maturity," I set about researching and compiling a list of famous "late bloomers." Actor Alan Rickman, Colonel Sanders, and Grandma Moses are just a few examples of people who didn't let conventional (limiting) beliefs about aging prevent them from taking concrete steps in pursuit of their dreams. Their stories gave me proof that it is never too late to reinvent oneself, develop hidden talents and ideas, and amass a fortune. My self-esteem was further buoyed by Robin McGraw's *What's Age Got to Do with It?* In this book, Robin fills the role of the warm, positive, and encouraging sister we all wish we had. She succeeds in convincing the reader that age has absolutely nothing to do with anything. I have thus been effectively inoculated against the inner "ageist" that was poised to start sapping me of self-esteem.

Great self-esteem can make all sorts of problems virtually disappear. Need proof? Try swapping high school yearbooks with someone you didn't know back then. Ask that person to pick two or three of the most attractive students in your graduating class. I can almost guarantee that his or her choices will not include the students deemed to be the most desirable or popular when you were in school. Plenty of average-looking or even objectively unattractive people are so transformed by high energy, charisma, and wit that they take on a believable perception of being highly attractive. Conversely, many shy introverts were actually true beauties who were hobbled by low self-esteem. No one even noticed that these people were beautiful because they didn't believe it themselves. Those who later manage to overcome their self-esteem issues are the "belles of the ball" at the twenty-year reunion.

People deemed to be attractive earn more than those who are deemed to be unattractive. Therefore, it makes sense to do what we reasonably can to improve and enhance our outward appearance. This outward appearance, though, is most dramatically improved and fueled by strong internal self-esteem. What can we do internally to increase our level of self-regard or self-love?

Again, drawing from experiences in working with more than ten thousand clients, I have come to believe that the key ingredient in self-esteem is character or personal integrity. Did you know that in the 1700s, the most popular type of self-help books focused on building one's character? This stands in stark contrast to themes popular in recent years. These tend to focus more on how to get what you want because you deserve it.

One personal character litmus test is whether you honor your commitments. Do you ever cancel an appointment at the eleventh hour just because you didn't feel like going? The other person may have believed your offered excuse or not. Their feelings may have been hurt or not. Your internal self-esteem, however, did most definitely suffer a nick. Every broken commitment or failed promise, no matter how small, has the effect of communicating to our own subconscious minds that we are untrustworthy. Our harshest critic lives within us. That critic sits in judgment when we fail to return borrowed items, fail to return the phone call of the annoying client or relative, or fail to attend a club or association meeting we signed up for. Too many of these slips will result in an outwardly noticeable lack of self-esteem. It is impossible to have real confidence and think well of ourselves when we have internal proof that we are unreliable or not worthy of people's confidence. Breaking too many promises will ultimately tear away at your self-esteem and thereby reduce your personal power.

What is the best way to avoid breaking commitments? Be super careful about what you agree to on the front end. At the risk of offending thousands of people whom I admire greatly, I readily admit that I would never in a million years agree to attend another Eagle Scout ceremony. This was always my least favorite event as an assemblywoman. None that I ever attended took less than three hours. I can remember sitting there seriously wondering whether being in a dentist's chair would be preferable. Nothing can possibly be worth the misery of sitting through the dozens of speeches by the youngsters' relatives, teachers, neighbors—the list went on and on and on. I'm sure that this public revelation will prevent another invitation from ever coming my way again. However, if invited, I will gladly give a card, a gift, or a letter, but I can't and won't give away three hours of my liberty again. Determining my bottom line, which is the second contracting step, causes me to assess what I am willing and unwilling to do and give in any situation. An honest evaluation enables me to politely but firmly decline invitations that I don't want to accept. Weakness and ambivalence, on the other hand, can cause me to say yes when I should have said no. We must know and respect our bottom line in order to preserve our personal power.

The habit of lying can also be a self-esteem robber. The lies I am referring to here are the small ones that many think are harmless. I don't think they are harmless, even if the person you are telling never knows the truth. Think about it. If I feel that I need to add something to a story to make it funny, I am really telling myself that I am not that funny or interesting on my own. I am positioning myself as being "less than" the person I'm talking to if I'm not "all that" on my own. It can be tempting to put additional cute words in your grandchild's mouth when recounting an anecdote. Did you think of a witty comeback that occurred to you only after an exchange? It can be tempting to include it in the retelling. It is best left out, however. This is because any tiny fib or exaggeration will allow the next one to come out more easily. Pretty soon there is a habit that can definitely erode one's self-esteem.

Why am I limiting my observations to small lies? People who tell big ones have problems way beyond a lack of self-esteem. Commenting on big liars is definitely above my pay grade. I have, however, known a lot of them. I remember an office worker who was a retired NYC cab driver. He had the best stories about dozens of celebrities who rode in his cab. Yes, it is entirely probable that a NYC cabbie has met a celebrity or two. But did Katharine Hepburn really invite "Abe" up to her apartment and then make lunch for him and Spencer Tracy? Was Eunice Shriver really in Abe's cab when news about JFK's assassination came across the radio? Maybe. But why were all of Abe's autographs in his own handwriting?

To the extent that poor self-esteem reduces one's earning potential and thereby reduces long-tem wealth prospects, then those little lies can definitely cost you.

Low self-esteem can also keep us stuck in personal relationships that don't serve us well. Being with the wrong person, in turn, can further erode one's self-esteem and sabotage wealth. I remember having one boyfriend who constantly criticized me. Within five minutes of picking me up to go somewhere, there would be a small insulting comment. "I didn't know people were still wearing those" or "I wouldn't have expected you to select that purse with your outfit." One of the interesting effects of the constant insults was that I spent (charged) a small fortune on new clothes. Looking back, I can see that I should have ended the relationship. At the time, however, my focus was on getting this person's approval. Seeking approval from a negative person in our inner circle is an exercise in futility. In my case, it was also expensive. My credit cards were all maxed out as I tried, in vain, to dress in a way that pleased my boyfriend. While stuck in a given situation, it can be difficult to see it clearly. Instead of ending the relationship, however, we engaged in endless discussions about whether and when to get married. In hindsight, I feel fortunate that "Robert" never wanted to set an actual wedding date. Instead, we went to couples counseling, where Robert and the therapist seemed focused on getting to the root cause of my "obsession" with setting a wedding date.

This was my first experience with using the contract process to deal with a personal issue. Step one of the contracting process caused me to determine "What do I want and need?" A: I wanted Robert to agree to set a date, get married, and have kids. Step two: What was I willing and unwilling to do in order to reach this goal? I realized that my focus on "setting a date" was probably having the exact opposite effect on Robert. I reasoned that he would be more inclined to want to set a date if I stopped bringing the subject up. But how long would I be willing to remain silent? The advice I received from many well-meaning friends was to give him an ultimatum. I realized then that the only ultimatum likely to be constructive was one I gave to myself. I realized that I couldn't change his behavior or mindset. The most I could do was to stop pressuring him and wait to see if that helped matters. But how long would I remain in that holding pattern? What was my bottom line? I knew that I had to draw a line in the sand that Robert couldn't know about. I decided to give it one year from the date I drew my mental line in the sand. Anything longer than this, I reasoned, would place my ultimate goal of getting married and having children in jeopardy.

And so it was that one year later, I ended the relationship. Robert wasn't exactly shocked (I suspect he was relieved) but suggested that we go back to the therapist to see what solutions he might offer. Robert conceded that the issue was with him, and he agreed to try to fix it. This would have been the collaboration or third step in the contracting process. How, though, could there be a successful negotiation and compromise solution between one party who wants to get married and another party who doesn't? Therapy to explore why Robert didn't want to get married seemed pointless to me. Almost as pointless as the previous inquiry into my "obsession" with setting a date. The fact was that he didn't want to get married and I did.

Perhaps therapy could have led to a "deal," but I was not willing to put my ultimate goal of getting married and having kids in jeopardy by spending more time in the familiar holding pattern that was our relationship.

The wealth-defeating effects of this relationship were twofold. As mentioned earlier, I was constantly shopping for new clothes in a futile attempt to be more attractive to Robert. Second, the amount of my waking time analyzing the relationship and speaking with friends about the relationship diverted me from the time and energy that might otherwise have been spent building my fledgling law practice. I wasn't freed up to creatively approach and enjoy this undertaking until after reassessing and reorganizing my personal life.

Roadblocks to wealth creation often come in the form of interpersonal relationships that do not serve us. The love contract process can be used to successfully deal with a whole host of relationship difficulties. However, I believe that deep down we know when we are in a relationship that can't be fixed. When that is the case, we will never be able to get out of our own way and on with the successful pursuit of happiness and wealth creation until we gracefully end the relationship.

There are no shortcuts to improving one's self esteem. Our inner judge knows everything we do and fail to do. I think it is impossible for me to "esteem myself" or love myself greatly if I allow someone to treat me poorly or if I treat someone else poorly. Eleanor Roosevelt hit the nail on the head when she said, "No one can make you feel inferior without your consent." In the context of a dead-end or abusive relationship, we have the ability to leave it. This may take a while, but it is within our power.

The trickier self-esteem robbers are negative people that we must endure either socially or in the workplace. These are the people who have a unique ability to make you feel "less than." The poster child for this type of person is the wife of a friend of mine. Her phony enthusiasm and air kiss upon greeting me are always followed by "You must be working too hard—you look sooo tired." *Ugh*. Everyone knows that is how women tell each other they look like shit while appearing to show concern. I can't cut off contact with this person at the risk of damaging other relationships that I do value. However, I am always "busy" when she suggests that we have lunch or go shopping. I have made a conscious choice not to eliminate her from my life. I have chosen, instead, to reduce and isolate my exposure to her. I treat her like car exhaust or secondhand smoke in that I just have to get through the encounter quickly enough for it to not harm me. When possible, eliminate your contact with self-esteem robbers. When this isn't possible, adopting a strategy of reducing and isolating contact can minimize damage to your precious self-esteem.

Our behavior toward others can have the biggest potential to either improve or derail self-esteem. Cutting someone off on the highway, for example, cannot help but lower my self-esteem. My brain has proof that I am a jerk. Small thoughtless acts such as failing to recycle or return the shopping cart in the grocery store parking lot will add up over time. It doesn't matter that no one else sees my bad behaviors—my internal judge, like Santa, knows if I've been bad or good. Over time, this translates directly into whether my brain believes I am worthy and deserving of all good things to come. I know that this sounds like it's heading in a New Age direction, but I guarantee you that your self-esteem will be boosted by treating others better. Try the following exercise for one day: Say nothing but positive things to other people. Through honest comments, positively delivered, endeavor to boost others up as a result of every exchange. Endeavor to leave each environment you encounter better that when you entered. This may be cleaning up a tiny bit more than the mess you made in the workplace cafeteria or folding a few more sweaters than the one you unfolded at the store. Most important, on this day, donate to your favorite charity. Whether through your time, your stuff, or your money, by helping people in need, you can join the ranks of the great people who make the world a better place.

Charitable giving may at first blush seem to be at odds with wealth creation. Throughout these pages, we have focused on eliminating external and internal drags on our wealth. This doesn't mean, however, that we shouldn't be charitable and share our wealth. The sharing that I counsel against is the involuntary type. I don't want you to have to "share" anything with exes, con artists, the government, and crazy relatives. We can and should, however, share with those in need. Amassing a big pile of loot for the exclusive com-fort, benefit, and amusement of oneself is, in my opinion, a rather pathetic and two-dimensional pursuit. On a fundamental level, we know that we should share some of what we have with others. Doing so causes us to have greater self-esteem and is associated with higher reported levels of personal happiness. We are also setting the right example for our children and grandchildren. By reducing unneces-sary spending on myself, and directing part of the freed-up money toward saving and investing and part of it toward helping others, we can come to know our own greatness. By doing the right thing with my wealth, I feel that I deserve it—and more! This mindset cannot fail to turbocharge our wealth-creation efforts.

Whenever young people ask me for career advice, I encourage them to get involved with a charitable organization. This is less "forced" than a networking group but can have the same desired effect of forging lasting personal, social, and professional alliances with like-minded people. Early on in one's career, the commodity we possess the most of is time. This is what we contribute to the charity at the outset. As time goes on, we tend to have more money than time. This is what we give our chosen organizations during our prime earning years. Last, we turn our attention to incorporating our charitable allies into our legacy planning. This can be done through our will and/or trust for an estate tax deduction. Those with estates below the current federal and state thresholds may wish to structure the charitable legacy as what's called a "precatory" gift to a child or other beneficiary.

For example, if I wish to leave $20,000 to the Red Cross, but my estate is currently less than the 2016 federal estate tax threshold of $5.4 million (assume that I don't live in a state with a separate estate tax), then the gift won't provide my estate with any tax benefits. How-ever, my will or trust can give the $20,000 to my daughter "with the hope that she sees fit to make a contribution in that amount to the Red Cross." Because the monies legally belong to my daughter at the time the gift is made, she will be entitled to an income tax deduction for the gift. See chapter 14 for more strategies to encourage future generations to continue charitable work.

Stress

Stress can also act as a wealth repellant. High stress levels contribute to physical ailments, substance abuse issues, lost time from work, and reduced productivity on the job. We all have different methods of dealing with stress in our lives. I implement a stress reducer or two in every SLC that I create. Looking at the big picture for a moment, I believe that the single most important thing that each of us can do to lower total societal stress is to stop being a cause of it to other people. Before your next meditation, tai chi, yoga, or aromatherapy session, give some thought to steps you might be able to take to stop causing stress for others.

In my house, the most stressful time of day is the morning rush to get ready for work and school. It is a daunting challenge for me to make breakfast and lunches, ensure that all items needed for after-school activities, permission slips, and homework assignments are packed, while also keeping the kids from dawdling to the point where they risk being late every single day. In that stressful morning vortex, I find it next to impossible to be a cheerful and supportive presence for the kids. I try very hard to keep my frustration levels in check. Otherwise, I know that I will feel guilty for the rest of the day and will not be working at an optimal level once in the office.

When not in the heat of the moment, I have tried repeatedly, but unsuccessfully, to tap into my natural bent for logic and organization. I have tried laying out the kids' clothes the night before, getting breakfast to the table a half hour earlier, playing upbeat music, and offering various rewards to the child ready by the front door first. Nothing worked. I quickly dismissed the fleeting idea of a cattle prod. Then, I took a shot at utilizing the contract process to deal with this problem.

1. *Q: What is it that I want?* A: A pleasant and stress-free morning and kids out the door on time.
2. *Q: What am I able and willing to do to bring this about?* A: I am willing to do anything to prevent my kids from being marked late at school. Thus far, however, none of my efforts

has proven capable of achieving both a pleasant breakfast and kids out the door on time. The morning stress levels? I am totally able to fix this, because I recognize that it all comes from me. The kids and husband are perfectly pleasant as they dawdle the morning away. Resolved that I can achieve 50 percent of the stated goal on my own, it is time for step three.

3. *Collaborate.* As I sit across the table from my fourteen- and ten-year-old, I state the problem as I see it and tell them what I am willing to do in an effort to have a more pleasant morning. I ask them what, if anything, they feel they are able to do to achieve a more pleasant morning while still being punctual. The responses are a few shrugs and seemingly half-hearted assurances that they will try. I realize then that they are not actually motivated to change their behavior to avoid being late because I have, thus far, shielded them from ever experiencing the natural consequences of their slow-motion mornings. The other party to this negotiation lacked information. They had no idea what it meant to be late because they never were late. I had been keeping them ignorant. That stopped the next morning.

To be fair, I gave them every opportunity to be on time. I showed them the clock on the wall and told them what time they needed to be done with breakfast in order to brush teeth, comb hair, tie shoes, etc. I also let them know that I would not be prodding them beyond one or two neutral reminders. It was a pleasant breakfast. They were also ten minutes late to school that day and were crushed to receive their first late passes. Was the result of this learning exercise perfectly pleasant and punctual mornings forevermore? Of course not. The difference, however, is that I see that they try to be on time, and more often than not, they succeed. For my part, I have gotten past the fear of my children being late, because I allowed it to happen. The earth didn't collapse. Do folks at school think that I am an imperfect parent because my kids are now late once in a while? Probably. And they are right. I am very far from perfect, but our mornings are much nicer.

Stress is a strong wealth repellant in several ways. It is huge drain on many household budgets. The costs of medication and self-medication can easily reach thousands of dollars per year. There are also countless costs in terms of lost opportunities. People who are dealing with a mountain of stress are probably not out there networking and optimizing their creativity to develop and build wealth. It is often all they can do to trudge to work each day, go through the motions, and then repeat the process the next day. Developing methods of effectively dealing with stress is essential for any of us who wish to get out of our own way in order to pursue our full wealth and human potential.

Coming up with effective tools to deal with stress will also enable us to better combat other wealth repellants. These tools include yoga, walking, running, meditation, and improved social interactions with others. Everyone needs to come up with his or her own best strategies. Just like physical pain, stress is a way that our body gives us information. The feeling of stress is a signal that something in our life is not quite right. It may be one's job, or it may involve dealing with a specific person at the job. Common sources of stress are personal relationships and finances. This is a catch-22, because stress has the effect of further depressing our finances. Whenever possible, we want to avoid the trap of treating the symptoms to the exclusion of the root cause of the stress. If, for example, I am stressed out because I am behind on holiday shopping or a deadline at work, it may be tempting to get a massage to deal with the stress. My time, however, is more effectively spent getting my task accomplished. I will then probably enjoy the massage more.

Takeaways

1. Force yourself to do something that frightens and/or embarrasses you (a little).
2. Eliminate white lies from what comes out of your mouth.
3. Do everything you can to boost others' feelings.
4. Give what you can to worthy charitable causes.
5. Experiment with a few stress-reducing activities and implement those that work.

12

THE LOVE CONTRACT IN ACTION

We know that breakups can be financially devastating. Does it then follow that staying in a broken relationship is the better financial decision?

Over the years, I have heard more than one attorney cynically advise a client contemplating divorce that it is "cheaper to keep her." This sounds plausible. If staying in an unhappy relationship can prevent the loss of half of one's assets, it arguably merits consideration. Without even getting into the definite emotional consequences of staying in a miserable relationship, I encourage my clients to give thought to the negative financial consequences of constant bickering that stops short of an actual breakup.

I have seen countless people who were effectively sapped of their wealth-building potential by the exhausting cycle of incessant "small" squabbles with their partners.

What is the effect on my happiness, discipline, and self-confidence of daily battles or simmering tensions with my partner? You can bet that it isn't positive. Can I effectively harness my creative energies in pursuit of wealth-building opportunities while at the same time experiencing the deadening effects of my partner's ever-expanding arsenal of idiosyncrasies, unkind acts, and general "weirdness"? I know from personal experience that staying in a relationship that can't be repaired does not help one's financial bottom line.

A relationship worthy of repair, however, can benefit tremendously by engaging in the love contract process. After years of using love contracts to protect my clients' assets, I began using them to deal with broader relationship and lifestyle irritations, pet peeves, and positive goals.

Beyond the threshold issues dealing with who gets what in the event of a split, this same document can be utilized to set forth your relationship goals and ideals. Think contracts are unromantic? If you are married, you are already living within a contract. You promised to "love, honor, and cherish" each other. The love contract can add some flesh to these bones by setting forth how you propose to accomplish the loving, honoring, and cherishing promises you made in your marriage contract. Utilizing the essential elements of a written legal contract provides a surprisingly effective tool by which couples can improve the quality of their relationships.

When something is important, we put it in writing. From to-do lists to New Year's resolutions, studies show that we are more inclined to remember and follow through with something if we put it in writing.

You wouldn't embark upon any other important venture or collaboration without a written document. Why then, when it comes to our most important venture, are we content to "wing it"?

Applying traditional contract theory and its process to a relationship in trouble takes much of the animus out of the equation by causing each party to first engage in some deep introspection. A great romance does not "just happen"—at least not after the first six months or so. One partner does not always "just know" what the other wants or what drives the other up the wall . . . On a more fundamental level, many of us have lost touch with what would truly make us happy, as individuals, let alone within a relationship. We are all so busy trying to make it through our increasingly hectic days that it is easy to lose touch with our spiritual and emotional lives. What on earth can a legal contract offer as a solution to these issues? Everything!

As we've seen already, at its core, a contract consists of several distinct phases. A party must first identify what it is that he or she wants. Within the context of the average contract, this is easy to answer: I want to buy that house, or I want to buy that antique desk. We wouldn't enter into a contract negotiation for something that we don't even want.

The second step causes us to ask what am I willing or unwilling to do or give in order to attain the goal. I may be happy and able to pay $150 for the antique desk. However, if the seller expects me to be responsible for transporting the item from Nebraska to New York, then we have a problem. In other words, what are my limits? If I agree to spend too much on the house or the desk, then I didn't do a very good job on step two. If I agreed to pay more than I can comfortably swing, then I have jeopardized my own security, and the results are not likely to be good. Remember, we are doing no one any favors if we compromise too much on the front end. Whether it is in the context of a love contract, buying a home, or my estate planning, if I give up my own security and protection going into a deal, then a bad result is far more likely to occur. I am again reminded of the airplane oxygen mask metaphor: we need to take care of ourselves first, or we are useless to everyone else.

Only after we have assessed our internal issues—determining what we want and what we are willing (and unwilling) to give in order to have it—can we then turn to our negotiating partner. Step three requires us to learn about the other party's desired outcome. How aligned is it with my desired outcome? How much flexibility does each side have? What are the consequences for deviation from the agreed-upon terms? And, last, what are the *deal breakers*?

Applying this process to the simplistic scenario of my desk, I first determine that I want it. I next determine that I am willing to pay $150 for it. However, when I move to the third step and try to create the deal with the seller, I learn that there is a huge stumbling block. I am unable to drive to Nebraska to pick the desk up. I am unwilling to pay to have the desk transported across the country. The shipping costs would likely be more than the cost of the desk. Are we at an impasse? Probably. It is still a good idea, though, to stay with the negotiation phase for a bit longer. I may learn that the seller has a trip to Massachusetts planned in two months and could bring the desk with him then. Am I willing to wait two months? Sure. Is the seller willing to bring the desk in his truck? Yes. However, he wants me to pay an additional $50 for lost-sale opportunities in the interim, as well as for the space it is currently taking up in his showroom. Only then will he hold it for me and transport it to the East Coast. I determine that I am unwilling to spend one-third of the desk price and am prepared to walk away. It might help to try another approach. I tell the seller that I am not prepared to pay the additional $50. But, if the desk isn't sold by the time that the seller is headed east, would he call me and we can make our original deal? This may or may not work out for me. However, I walk away secure in the knowledge that I was reasonable, creative, and, most important, true to myself. I didn't bend too far trying to reach an agreement.

Yes, the desk metaphor is somewhat simplistic. Should I and would I be more willing to bend in the context of my interpersonal relationships? Of course. I should just always be mindful of the dangers of bending too far.

Every contract has consequences for failed performance. The level of penalty to be agreed upon should correspond to the perceived severity of the infraction. For example, if a borrower makes a mortgage payment three weeks late, there is a late charge imposed by the bank. This relatively minor consequence is part of the contract that the borrower and bank agreed to. If the borrower is three months late paying the mortgage, the consequences are much more serious. This, too, was agreed upon in advance by both parties.

The parties to an LC are free to choose fun, nonlegally binding penalties for small "pet peeve" violations. These may consist of paying quarters into a charity jar or having to wear a sandwich board at a local shopping center. Bigger infractions such as the contract's enumerated deal breakers may be dealt with by way of more severe, legally binding penalties.

Choice of arbiter: the default arbiter for love contract disputes is ultimately a court of law in the parties' county of domicile. The couple may also select an alternative dispute resolution mechanism. This can be a friend or a professional. I am sometimes called upon to referee LC disputes.

Pet Peeves

Minor annoyances, over time, can have very destructive consequences. The love contract process asks us to list, but not share, all of the other person's annoying habits. We then remove from the list those items that are beyond the other person's control. An example might be a deviated septum that results in snorting or frequent coughing. The issues beyond the other's control should be placed on our own personal SLC. For example: "I will work on feeling compassion for Harry and gratitude that my airway is not similarly obstructed."

Of the items that remain on the list, try narrowing them down to two or three. It is important that each party have the same number of pet-peeve items. These gripes are then incorporated into the love contract. Try hard to be objective and neutral sounding in your characterization. For example, "I sometimes feel unsafe when we are driving" sounds less accusatory than "Have you considered taking driving lessons?"

By incorporating your pet peeves into the love contract, you are freed up from the constant need to verbalize these points. You can take the moral high ground knowing that a regular review of the contract will cause the other party to know where he or she has veered off track. This allows the parties to "outsource the nagging."

Embarking on Your First Love Contract

Think of your first love contract as your mission statement as a couple. It can be a tool to help you, as a couple, design or redesign your life together. What do you want your joint life to look like? The initial categories that most love contracts include are fitness, adventure, wealth, culture, philanthropy, social life, and, finally, pet peeves and disagreements.

Each party should first give thought to perceived deficiencies in each area and how they would like to see themselves one year out. The following are sample categories in a love contract.

FITNESS

Looking back at the past year, have we become too sedentary? Modern technology has freed us up from many strenuous chores performed by our ancestors. We no longer have to roll up the carpets and drag them into the backyard to beat them. We no longer have to carry water into the house from a well. The list of now obsolete labors from days gone by is seemingly endless. The ironic result of this is that we are now faced with the dilemma of having to create artificial work for our bodies in the form of exercise. We are at a little disadvantage here compared to our ancestors. Without their daily labors, family life would have come to a halt. For us, our "artificial work" in the form of exercise is optional on any given day. If I fail to go to the gym or out for a jog, my family will not starve. Over the long term, however, a sedentary lifestyle has been linked to shorter life expectancies and many other negative health and mood consequences.

Do we both want to adopt a more active lifestyle? What one thing can we incorporate into our weekly routine to get more exercise together? A weekend morning hike at a nearby park? A yoga class or DVD? Tennis instruction? Tango lessons? A weekend bike ride? Roller skating? Bowling?

Daily baseline exercise is usually pursued separately (SLC items), given most couples' work schedules. But committing to engage in at least one joint activity per week will add to your total activity level while shaking up your routine a bit. Joint pursuit of a fitness goal makes it more likely that you will stick with it. Even a small team of two can provide motivation and encouragement that an individual doesn't benefit from.

Next, what is one unhealthy habit that you can delete or reduce? If evenings after work are spent in front of the TV with snacks, maybe the frequency can be reduced? Ideally, the selection of the fitness goal will be doubly beneficial in that the weekly activity will necessarily reduce time on the couch.

ADVENTURE

To combat the inevitable emergence of boredom within our relationships and lives, the love contract should include at least one aspirational action/adventure item per year. Both parties should separately list five things they would be willing to try and then compare notes. Zip-lining? Kayaking? A group bicycle vacation? Whitewater rafting? Whale watching? The anticipation of experiencing a new activity is a definite tonic for a couple.

CULTURE

To get out of our little ruts, the love contract should include at least one cultural pursuit. This should be something that both parties want to do. Having coerced more than one partner to sit through a ballet against his will, I know that this is one of my loves best pursued alone or with friends (SLC item). What activity would you both enjoy? A play? Museum? Symphony? By jointly experiencing the highest levels of human talent, our small silly and petty conflicts can be placed in proper perspective.

SOCIAL LIFE

People with strong friendships live longer and report higher levels of happiness. Strong social networks also facilitate wealth building. Our crazed schedules, however, could have a dampening effect on our ability to create, nurture, and maintain friendships. Housewives having morning coffee after the husband and kids have left seems like a quaint vestige from "Mayberry" life. Today, I don't even know all of my neighbors' names. Spending time with other couples is important, because it gives us the ability to put our own little squabbles into perspective.

Each partner should separately think of three other couples you would like to invite over for dinner, drinks, or game night. Then compare lists. Each love contract should include the names of a couple that you agree to spend some more time with.

This section of the love contract may also focus on pulling back from relationships that do not serve you well as a couple. These may include incessant braggarts and negative people as well as those who indulge in behaviors that you as a couple have left in the past.

PHILANTHROPY

To powerfully elevate the plane of one's relationship, I strongly recommend pursuing at least one joint philanthropic goal every year. This can be done as a couple or as a family. Options for inclusion are a service vacation, monthly sponsorship of a child, organizing or participating in a Valentines for Veterans drive, or bringing toys to a homeless shelter or battered women's shelter. There are so many worthy options. Some preliminary research is in order to avoid being scammed. There are some sham charities. There are also, unfortunately, many perfectly legal organizations that spend most of the money collected on salaries and administrative expenses. Before making a donation, check the organization out on www.charitynavigator.org to see what percentage of each dollar collected actually makes its way to those in need. Helping others, as a couple, can have the effect of reducing the significance of your own trials and tribulations while casting your partner in a whole new light.

WEALTH

Being part of a couple can make it easier to build wealth if both partners are actively working toward this as a joint goal. Each love contract should include at least one wealth-building exercise or project. I worked with one couple who purchased a vacation home every year. They would spend weekends renovating, painting, and landscaping the property. At the conclusion of this process, they would list the house for sale and then buy a new property. They enjoyed the projects because they lived in the properties while they worked and always selected interesting locations that enabled them to explore the countryside in their downtime. This particular wealth-building exercise wouldn't work for me because I have absolutely no renovation talents or ability. Another type of wealth-building exercise that might be included in a love contract is an education item. Perhaps we can take a class on investments or estate planning to learn more about building and protecting our nest egg. Or we can pursue something more creative such as a class on furniture upholstery or refinishing. Both skill sets lend themselves to a side business capable of generating a respectable cash flow with which to invest.

If the love contract process is being used as a mission statement or life redesign tool, then the wealth category will focus on methods of eliminating unnecessary spending and building wealth. A couple may also wish to include property distribution "exit rules" if the relationship is in serious trouble, if one of the parties is required to have a traditional prenuptial agreement pursuant to the terms of a corporate governance document, or if an inheritance for one of the partners is conditioned upon having a prenup, postnup, or cohab. It is much easier to broach the property distribution discussion if it is done as part of a broader dialogue and goal-setting process.

MICHAEL AND ANITA'S STORY

Michael and Anita had a few financial problems within their relationship. Michael grew up in poverty, worked incredibly hard for many years, and went on to own ten successful toy stores. Prior to meeting Anita, he went through two nearly financially ruinous divorces. He didn't have a prenuptial agreement in place prior to entering into the first two marriages. He vowed never to get married again. When he and Anita met, he was very clear about never wanting to get married. He thought being honest with her was the right thing to do. Anita persevered. She loved Michael and was determined to wait it out. She had seen more than one high-profile individual vow to never get married again only to reverse course after a few years. Anita then became pregnant. Michael still wasn't biting. However, one year after their daughter was born, Michael felt that he was ready to marry Anita, provided that she sign an ironclad prenuptial agreement. She agreed, and they have been pretty happy for the past several years with the exception of some financial issues. Michael feels that Anita spends too much money. Her spending on their pets particularly frustrates him. Anita is exasperated that several years into the marriage, Michael still isn't comfortable putting her name on any asset, including the home in which they live. Here are some of the love contract clauses we created in order to help them deal with these issues:

ARTICLE 6: FINANCES

Each party seeks to strengthen their financial position. Anita's financial goals include buying a beach house and paying off her credit card debt. Michael's financial goals include buying a boat and reducing total household debt. To these ends, the parties have agreed to take steps to reduce spending and make the following requests of the other party:

6.1 Michael requests that Anita reduce her discretionary spending to no more than $1,000 per month. Expenses related to the rescue dogs will count against this "allowance."

6.2 Anita agrees not to adopt any more rescue animals, and she further agrees never again to invade a retirement account to pay for medical care and/or treatment of the rescue animals.

6.3 Anita requests that Michael refrain from hiding assets or placing assets in another person's name.

6.4 Anita realizes that Michael's insecurities about finances stem, in part, from growing up in poverty and having gone through several costly divorces. Nevertheless, she aspires to achieving a level of trust and confidence that will allow Michael to add her name to more of the assets that he brought into the marriage.

6.5 Michael agrees to discuss putting Anita's name on the house once she has reduced her outstanding credit card debt to less than $5,000.

6.6 Both parties agree to attend a financial education class at their local community college.

6.7 Michael agrees that his support of his adult children from his first marriage has imposed a strain on household finances. He hereby agrees to limit his support and/or gifts to his adult children to no more than $500.00 per month. He further agrees that he will not pay for more than one wedding for each of his three adult children.

6.8 Each party agrees to investigate long-term care insurance options to safeguard their assets from future possible long-term care expenses.

Note the aspirational format of 6.4. No one is holding a gun to Michael's head, requiring him to put Anita's name on assets. She realizes that she agreed within the prenup that assets would remain separate. However, at this point, she feels sort of like a second-class citizen in that he owns everything and she owns nothing. Michael explained to me that he would feel more comfortable entrusting Anita with some portion of the assets if he saw her acting more responsibly with household finances. I also urged Anita, within an SLC, to boost her own wealth-building capacity. If Michael could start with nothing and

become wealthy, why couldn't she? Anita is beautiful,
smart, and charming. I encouraged her to think about
possible career options now that their daughter is in
school. Anita is now working toward interior design
certification at a local college. Michael now feels
a bit less anxious knowing that Anita aspires to one
day earn money as opposed to simply spending what he
earns.

DEAL BREAKERS

Within each love contract, the parties may wish to include one or
two actions or behaviors that would likely have the effect of ending
the relationship. These items may be gleaned from past behavior. If,
for example, I somehow managed to survive a prior episode of infidelity, I will want to put the offending party on notice that I am very
much inclined to bolt in the event of a relapse.

Now that every state in the United States has no-fault divorce,
everyone is free to leave a marriage for any reason or no reason at all.
Therefore, if there are things that you know you would have a great
deal of difficulty getting past, then it is a matter of fundamental fairness to let your partner know. These serious issues can include infidelity, substance relapses, physical abuse, gambling, or gender reassignment. Labeling anything as a deal breaker does not definitively
mean that I will leave if it occurs. It simply means that there is a very
realistic possibility that I will not be able to get past it.

PET PEEVES

The love contract provides a very effective mechanism for dealing
with pet peeves because it comprises but a small part of a broader,
nobler, and enlightened mission-statement-type document and process. Because it comes last in the process, it seems to be a relatively
small afterthought. The discussion of pet peeves comes only after we

formulate health, fitness, wealth, philanthropy, and other life redesign action steps. Each party seemingly lists a few pet peeves only because the love contract process requires them to do so. The fact that certain behaviors annoy you to the point where you want to scream is not readily apparent to your partner. The upshot is that chances for an amicable resolution are greater when the topic is presented neutrally and as a part of a broader process. There is something now requiring me to give voice to the things that I've been bearing while trying very hard to grin. The following love contract case studies deal with specific pet peeves experienced by my clients and myself, together with negotiated solutions that worked with varying degrees of success. Hopefully, these case studies will have the effect of putting your grievances in perspective, while giving you some ideas to begin your own love contract.

Within the Pet Peeve section of your love contract, I recommend trying to anticipate what your partner will list as his or her pet peeves regarding your behavior.

This can add some levity to the exchange with your partner in step three of the contract process.

Love Contract for Physical or Cosmetic Enhancement

It's also possible to have your love contract deal with plastic or cosmetic surgeries.

JILL AND CHRIS'S STORY

Jill was extremely anxious about the possibility that her husband, Chris, would one day leave her for a younger woman. This happened with her first husband, and she was determined not to let it happen again.

In an attempt to remain attractive, Jill has undergone many plastic-surgery procedures. She has had breast augmentation, a tummy tuck, a brow lift, and what was described by her doctor as a "mini" face lift. In between the actual surgical procedures, Jill has had minor procedures such as botox, various injectable fillers, and chemical peels.

Her pursuit of the fountain of youth has become a big financial drain on the family. However, because she handles all the finances, it's been relatively easy to keep the magnitude of her cosmetic spending beneath the radar. Chris thinks the reason they're short on cash is that his daughter from a prior marriage, Suzanna, has just started college. Jill asked Chris to sign off on a home equity line of credit, explaining that it was needed to pay Suzanna's tuition. The reality is that Jill plans to use the money for more plastic surgery—this time butt implants.

One evening, Jill inadvertently left the credit card statements and checkbook on the kitchen table. Chris had a look and felt short of breath when he realized what bad shape they were in. He saw that more was spent on doctor bills than Suzanna's tuition. A fiery confrontation ensued. Jill came clean about the extent of her cosmetic-enhancement spending as well as her intended use of the money pulled from the home equity line of credit.

Chris's initial reaction was to leave the marriage. This was bitterly ironic for Jill, because she underwent all of the costly procedures in an attempt to keep Chris from leaving. On the recommendation of a friend, they decided to give the love contract process a try.

After a preliminary phone call with Jill and Chris, it was clear to me that they needed separate attorneys. Because I represented Jill in the couple's prenuptial agreement five years earlier, she remained my client in the LC process. Chris asked his friend and real estate attorney if he could help him with this type of contract. The attorney thought it was a joke at first but agreed to engage in the process as a courtesy to his good friend.

We each met with the parties separately. Jill admitted to me that her spending had gotten out of control. However, she also told me that Chris spends nearly as much as he makes on his three Harleys, pricy leather jackets, boots, and other biker accoutrements. He also spends heavily on sports memorabilia. Jill believes Chris is also to blame for driving the family to financial ruin.

The parties consented to having the sessions recorded. The following are excerpts from my solo meeting with Chris's attorney, Sol:

Sol: This is bad. They need miracle workers instead of lawyers. Their levels of dysfunction, however, seem perfectly matched. I'll tell you up front that Chris will bail unless she agrees to stop the cosmetic madness. I've seen the receipts. It's insane.

Ann: Jill doesn't deny that she has had a few costly procedures.

Sol: A few?! She can't close one of her eyes for crying out loud! She's had two rounds of breast implants, a facelift, a tummy tuck, and liposuction—to name a few! They are on the verge of bankruptcy over this. Now she wants to use the home equity line of credit that she tricked him into to pay for butt implants. I can tell you right now this is a deal breaker for Chris.

Ann: He agreed to the loan. He knew exactly what he was signing.

Sol: Yeah—you're leaving out one tiny detail. He was under the misapprehension that the loan was to pay for his daughter's college! Where could he have come up with that idea? Any guesses?

Ann: Jill will gladly use the home equity money to pay for Suzanna's tuition. She has no problem with

*that—she just wants to use some of the money to
improve her appearance.*

Sol: *Well, her efforts are counterproductive. Chris
thinks she's starting to look like a mannequin. I
have to tell you, I don't disagree with him. What
normal person would risk bankruptcy in order to
have plastic surgery that is starting to make her
look like a freak?*

Ann: *Your client could also use some personal finance
self-control. He spends more on baseball memorabilia than she does on her appearance.*

Sol: *The baseball collection is worth something!*

Ann: *I have news for you—Jill had it appraised and it
isn't even worth what he spent on it. I don't even
know where to start on this love contract.*

Sol: *For starters, she needs to agree to end her
obsession with plastic surgery. Perhaps some therapy would be useful to alleviate her obvious inse-
curity over her looks and fear of being left.*

Ann: *Wow, you really sound like a male chauvinist.
Has it occurred to you that there may be aspects
of Chris's behavior that cause her to be insecure?
Perhaps if he paid more attention to her and spent
less time in the basement with his baseball cards,
that would help. Maybe a joint activity would help
them—like joining a gym? This might help Jill feel
more confident about her appearance and also allow
them to spend some time together. Not to be rude,
but he could stand to hit the gym a bit. . . . What
do you think?*

Sol. *That's a fair start, but it doesn't address her
expensive penchant for cosmetic procedures. She
needs to agree to stop.*

Ann: *That's not realistic. Today, many of these procedures aren't even considered as invasive as having*

your hair colored. I think she should be free to
continue the chemical peels and Botox injections.
Sol: So, what's the compromise here? The butt implant
thing has Chris ready to blow a gasket. He believes
this spending will deprive Suzanna of her tuition
money. "Daughter's education versus wife's booty."
What choice do you think Chris and Jill should
make?
Ann: Point well taken. Perhaps the stair climber at
the gym will help the butt issue. If she agrees not
to get the new glutes, will he give her a break
with the minor procedures?
Sol: What can she do to keep the costs down? Perhaps
she can have the procedures done at a school by
students?
Ann: I can't agree to let students perform surgery
on my client. I can, however, assure you that she
will agree within the love contract to good faith
efforts to reduce the cosmetic expenditures.
Sol: How?
Ann: She will agree to comparison shop and to reduce
the frequency of the procedures. Again, surgery by
students is a nonstarter. Can Chris cool it with
the baseball collection? Maybe he can sell a few
of them to generate some money for the household?
Sol: I'm not sure that he is willing to part with any
of the cards. I will ask, though. How long does he
need to go without buying new cards?
Ann: Till Suzanna is done with school?
Sol: Deal. What about requiring that they go to therapy within the love contract?
Ann: Let's leave that up to them. Therapy may be helpful, but the more immediate issue for both of them
is to stop these behaviors that are pushing them
apart.

> *Sol: OK, what do we have?*
> *Ann: Jill will agree to forego the butt implant.*
> *Sol: Chris will take a break from acquiring more base-*
> *ball memorabilia.*
> *Ann: They will join a gym, and Jill can continue with*
> *her minor appearance enhancements.*
> *Sol: Provided that she seeks to keep the costs down.*
> *Ann: And they agree to check back with us in three*
> *months to see how it's going. Deal?*
> *Sol: Deal. Write it up!*
> This dialogue came from an actual love contract nego-
> tiation.

One may ask why Chris and Jill needed outsiders—lawyers no less—to get involved and hammer out something that on its surface seems so straightforward and logical. Anyone in a relationship may be able to appreciate the fact that logic can often take a backseat to an endless dispute loop between the parties. Employing the legal process with its tried-and-true structure has the effect of removing animus from the equation. I also find that the presence of neutral and objective outsiders tends to elicit more reasonable positions from the parties.

The love contract process is not a therapy session. The parties may or may not also engage in actual couples counseling. The contract process is different from therapy or counseling. The contract simply requires the couple to agree to ground rules to eliminate or reduce behavior that infuriates the other. We agree to stop doing X, Y, or Z, and the other party agrees to do or stop doing A, B, or C. The couple may or may not also wish to try to figure out, in therapy, why they are doing X, Y, or Z. If, for example, one party recognizes a pattern of certain behavior or if he has heard similar complaints in past relationships, then he may wish to find out why this keeps happening. This inquiry may well constitute an action item on someone's next solo love contract.

Love Contract with a Slob

After ensuring that I am doing everything within my power to positively affect my surroundings (see chapter 10), I can now turn my
attention to my partner's efforts in this area. When one partner values organization and orderliness more than the other does, this can
be a big source of conflict. I continuously struggle with this in my
marriage. Applying the LC process to myself, I ask, "What is it that
I truly want and need? Answer: "Beautiful and orderly surroundings." Next, what am I willing and unwilling to do or give in order
to attain my goal? As it relates to myself, I have this area of my life
wired. I have a dizzying number of personal organization rules by
which I live. These behaviors may well merit a diagnosis by a mental
health professional. In any event, if I lived alone, my home would be
a beacon of organization. Alas, I have "roomies" in the form of two
dogs, two sons, and a husband. The dogs are probably the neatest of
the bunch. The boys are the messiest but are most easily dealt with.
When they are home, there are always TV shows and video games to
barter with. When they're not home, I whip out my two black garbage bags and organize away. The husband, however, is a tricky one.

Invoking the LC process: What do I want? Organization! What
am I willing to do to get it? Anything! If he isn't organized, I will not
only lead by example, I will organize his stuff for him.

ANN'S STORY

During our first year of marriage, I thought that I
would surprise Bill by decluttering his closet, which
was so crammed with junk that it couldn't close. I dutifully filled one bag with clothing that needed tailor-
ing. Why would someone rehang shirts missing buttons
or a jacket that needed a new zipper? There was a bag
for charity donations. If I hadn't seen him wear an
item in the time that I knew him, into the charity bag
it went. That is, with the exception of clothing that

was in such bad shape that I wouldn't risk offending a charitable recipient. Items beyond repair went into the garbage bag. The rust-colored parachute pants and single Capezio dance shoe? Trash bag for sure! He was definitely lucky to have me around. Stacks of medical journals that I knew he'd never get around to reading? I decided to throw out any of them that were more than two years old. The research and articles must surely be outdated by now. I was probably saving him from a lawsuit. In less than an hour, I beheld the results of my logical and disciplined labors. I couldn't wait for him to get home!

I can probably count, on one hand, the number of serious arguments that Bill and I have had over the years. I can't even say that I remember them well—with the exception of that first fight over that #@%!ing closet. My handsome, articulate, and charming husband looked and sounded like King Kong when he saw that closet. The takeaway for me was that my efforts to organize him would never be well received. I have come to accept that he has an inexplicable need to hang onto things like matchbooks, golf balls, golf score cards, old calendars, pieces of twine, broken sunglasses, old cell phones, broken stethoscopes, socks with holes, and surgical gloves—to name but a few.

What is our LC step-three collaborative solution? I want and need to be in an organized environment. I have come to understand that he wants and needs to hang onto a lot of debris. (I don't understand why, but that isn't important here.) I now get that I can't throw his stuff out. But I don't want to live on the set of *Sanford and Son* either. The solution? Why, an attractive basket with a closing lid from Pottery Barn! He can keep whatever he wants in there, and I don't have to see it. Problem solved. It was for a few

months, anyway. Then the stuff began to spill over the
basket. Next solution? A bigger basket! We are on our
fourth basket. The next one may have to be as large
as his dresser.

I know some people who object to their partner leaving their
socks on the floor wherever they take them off. I wish Bill did that.
Instead, he makes a half-hearted attempt to pitch them in the general direction of the hamper. The problem is that the dry-cleaning
bag is next to the hamper. I don't always get around to fishing the
errant sock or pair of underwear from the dry cleaning bag in time.
All too often the dry cleaning is delivered back to the house with a
single sock or pair of underwear draped over a hanger and wrapped
in plastic at a cost of $3.50. I imagine that they are puzzled at the
eccentrics who send underwear with holes to be dry-cleaned. This is
but one example of how being disorganized can cost a couple money.
My short-term fix is to keep the dry cleaning bag in another room.

As I continue to struggle with finding clever solutions to our
organizational challenges, it has occurred to me that I have not really
been following my own LC process. For example, the collaboration
required by step three? Yes, I do take my husband's bottom line (he
needs his collection of junk) into account. But I then proceed to
come up with the fix with no input from him. Maybe he has no
input to give, but I recognize that I've never really asked him if he
has any suggested solutions. I realize that in any joint negotiation or
problem solving, both sides will be more invested in the outcome if
they have each had meaningful contributions. On this clause, we will
head back to the negotiating table.

FINANCIAL INFIDELITY

In response to a recent survey by Bankrate.com, more than seven
million people admitted to keeping financial secrets from their partners. Left unchecked, financial secrets can compromise a couple's

long-term security while also eroding the very fabric of their relationship.

Prior to employing a love contract to deal with financial infidelity, one must first determine whether a partner is keeping secrets.

Spotting Financial Infidelity

The biggest clue to financial infidelity is a PO box key that you didn't know about. This indicates that mail is being concealed. More often than not, this hidden mail includes financial statements or credit card bills.

Information can also be revealed by running your credit scores at least once a year. This may well force the issue out into the open if big surprises are revealed.

Look at the credit card statements for purchases of gift cards. Gift cards are sometimes used to purchase gifts for third parties without a direct description of the gift on the credit card statement. Also check the credit card statement or other bills for overpayments. These are sometimes made with the intention of requesting a refund that one partner knows nothing about.

Once you are pretty sure that you have identified financial infidelity, you are ready to embark upon the love contract process to deal with it.

Step one calls for us to look inward and determine what we want from the situation. Do we want out of the relationship, or do we want to attempt to fix the problem and move forward as a couple? Is your goal to strengthen your future financial security? If you still believe in and want to pursue a joint future, then proceed to step two.

Step two calls for us to elucidate what it is that we are willing and unwilling to do individually in order to address the problem. Yes, it is tempting to shout angry accusations and throw the evidence of financial infidelity at our partner, but this will probably not get me any closer to my stated goal. Instead, am I willing to be honest about my own financial secrets? We all have a few. I admit that on more than one occasion, when asked if clothing was new, I responded,

"This? Oh no, it's been in the back of my closet forever!" Harmless? Maybe. But before embarking on an angry confrontation, it is helpful to shine the interrogation lamp on ourselves. Step two should also help us try to understand what might be behind the secret spending or savings. I said earlier that the LC process is not a therapy session. This doesn't mean that I shouldn't try to understand my partner's motivations. Does he have financial baggage from childhood? Is he using the money to help his parents or adult children who are having a hard time?

Step three is the joint discussion or collaboration. I recommend that the party leading the charge begin by expressing his or her long-term financial goals. This may be acquiring a vacation house or amassing the money needed to start a dream business. Next, acknowledge how you may need to be more open about your separate spending in preparation for establishing some joint written financial goals in the LC. I have found that this approach is the one least likely to result in in a pointless spiraling argument.

CROSS-DRESSING

Caitlyn Jenner's public reveal has made millions of people more comfortable with gender identification issues. That doesn't mean that these are quite yet easy issues for couples and families to deal with.

```
            DENISE AND PETER'S STORY

My client Denise called me for legal advice prior to
leaving her husband, Peter. She knew that Peter had
dressed as a woman for years, at home and outside of
the presence of the kids. She never quite got used to
this but rationalized that it was a harmless way for
Peter "to let off some steam." Lately, though, he has
been going to the supermarket and picking the kids up
from school dressed as "Raquel." He even hinted at
```

the possibility of going to work as Raquel. Peter is
a plumber.

In response to a few questions, Denise told me that
she would be inclined to stay with Peter but couldn't
be in a relationship with someone willing to embarrass
her in public and whose sexual orientation she was
unsure of.

Though not overwhelmingly positive, Denise's statement indicated that there was a scenario in which she
could still imagine the possibility of a joint future
with Peter. Though tentative, this was enough of a step
one response to merit an exploration of the other LC
steps.

Step two elicited a quick response from Denise.
She was very definitely unwilling to go out with Peter
dressed as Raquel. What was she willing to do? This
was harder. Why should she have to be willing to do
anything? After all, it wasn't anything she did that
was causing the problems. Perhaps not. Was she willing, though, to at least educate herself about the
practice and prevalence of cross-dressing?

Denise met with a therapist who specializes in
gender identity issues. She learned that there are no
real reliable statistics, because so many cross-dress-
ers still keep the practice secret. The therapist did
assure Denise that cross-dressing in and of itself did
not have any bearing upon one's sexual orientation. It
was entirely possible and, in the therapist's opinion,
probable that Peter was heterosexual. Denise proceeded
to read *Cross Dress for Success* by Veronica Vera to
learn more. While she still had no more of an idea of
why Peter would want to dress like a woman, her tiny
education had the effect of destigmatizing the practice: Peter sure seemed to have a lot of company out
there.

In step three, Denise and Peter sat down to see what could be worked out. In an effort to make Peter feel less self-conscious, Denise revealed some fetish-type behavior of her own. Peter asked if she could learn to accept his need to go out in public as Raquel. He explained that after spending so many hours on clothing and makeup, he wanted to show his special side to the world. She did understand this but asked him to consider the feelings of their teenaged sons, who were being teased at school. If Denise agreed to periodically have lunch or dinner with Raquel, could Peter agree to keep Raquel from picking the kids up from school or sports practices? We cobbled together a few rules to include in their LC and are scheduled to assess progress in three months.

Could Peter and Denise have come up with these compromise rules without involving me or a written contract? Sure. However, I don't think they would have. It was only by involving "outsiders" in the process that Denise was able to come to accept that Peter was not necessarily a "weirdo" whom she couldn't fathom staying with. Again, the tried-and-true contract process removed the aimless finger pointing and recriminations.

By focusing on the contract process with its individual steps, we are out of the blame game and on track to forge a workable solution.

INFIDELITY IN THE RELATIONSHIP

One of the most common reasons for all breakups is cheating by one of the parties. There is no magical formula by which any type of contract or agreement can prevent someone from cheating. I do believe, though, that the love contract process provides a mechanism with which partners can attempt to cobble together a framework to move forward if they choose to do so.

LOUIE AND MARIE'S STORY

Louie and Marie were infidelity "survivors." Lou was a drug rep for a pharmaceutical company and was on the road a lot. As a top seller, he was often rewarded with seminars and vacations in resort locations. Marie accompanied him when she could but often had to stay home with their three young children. The couple's mutual friend Connie was also a drug rep who went on many of the same trips as Louie. During an outdoor cocktail party on a recent trip, Connie came upon Louie strolling on the beach hand in hand with a woman she had never seen. During dinner, she told Louie in no uncertain terms that if he didn't tell Marie, she would.

After months of therapy, the couple was back on solid footing. They agreed that Louie's extensive travel schedule needed to stop. In an attempt to save his marriage, Louie quit his job as a drug rep and took an office job with an insurance company. Things were much better now that he was home more.

Two years later, though, Marie discovered proof that Louie had strayed again, this time with his secretary at the insurance company. Marie had pretty much had it at this point but, having grown up in a single-parent household, was very reluctant to disrupt her kids' lives with a divorce.

Marie came to me for a postnuptial agreement. She was staying in the marriage for the moment but wanted to work out the couple's financial settlement ahead of time, in the event that the latest reconciliation did not work out. One's negotiating position is usually at its strongest when the other party is groveling. I asked Marie if she wanted to include a penalty clause. In other words, Marie would be entitled to an extra payment if Louie strayed again, prior to a possible divorce. They both agreed to a $50,000 payment to the aggrieved party for any future episode of infidelity.

I then asked the couple if they were interested in including any type of lifestyle provisions in the contract to try to reduce the chances of another episode of infidelity. While Marie recognized that Louie would either remain faithful or not and knew she couldn't do much to control the outcome, she did have one request. She asked Louie to agree that he would not hire any new female secretary or assistant unless she was at least fifty pounds overweight and unattractive, as determined by Marie. She was essentially asking for veto power over all future new hires in Louie's office.

While I believe Louie would have agreed to anything at that point, he readily agreed to allow Marie to have final say on hiring his direct assistants. I know other couples who employ this strategy when hiring housekeepers and nannies who live in the household. In the wake of Gwen Stefani's and Jennifer Garner's divorces, I have been asked to draft more than a few "Ugly Nanny" clauses.

There are several variations on clauses designed to reduce straying. The following is an actual clause I drafted for a stay-at-home dad and his high-powered jet-setting wife:

ARTICLE 3. JEALOUSIES/TEMPTATIONS

3.1 Friends of the opposite sex. The parties encourage each other to develop and maintain a wide variety of friendships and collegial relationships. However, in an attempt to reduce the likelihood of dangerous temptations as well as the public appearance of impropriety, the following rules are agreed to:

  a. Personal trainers engaged by either party shall be deemed to be no more attractive to the other party than a "7" on a scale of 1 to 10.

  b. Laura shall discourage solo business dinners with male coworkers whose appearance Andrew deems to be "7" or greater on a scale of 1 to 10.

  c. Laura acknowledges that Andrew has no choice but to spend a fair amount of time with mothers of the kids' classmates at both morning drop-off and afternoon pick-up. He occasionally has coffee with the group. He hereby agrees not to have coffee alone with any mother whose appearance is deemed by Laura to be a "7" or greater on a scale of 1 to 10.

Some infidelity clauses lay out monitoring methods to ensure compliance as well as specific sanctions that can be imposed, whether the couple breaks up or not. Here is an example:

ARTICLE 1: FIDELITY

Each party hereby reaffirms their commitment that they will be 100 percent faithful to the other. Measures to ascertain compliance with this requirement may include enlisting a private detective. Each party agrees to this. Each party also hereby agrees to submit to an annual polygraph test only if requested to do so by the other party.

ARTICLE 2: SANCTIONS

In the event that either party is unfaithful to the other, then and in that event, the offending party shall execute a deed transferring of his or her one-half ownership of the marital residence, located at 123 Cherry Tree Drive, Ronkonkoma, New York (or replacement residence) to the other party. This sanction shall be imposed whether or not the parties actually divorce. In addition to the marital home, the offending party shall forfeit all household property, furnishings, china, glassware, silverware, and decorative objects. Excluded from this shall be the offending party's own clothing, toiletries, jewelry, and objects of personal adornment.

THE WEIGHT CLAUSE

Way back in time, when Jessica Simpson and Tony Romo were engaged, they were rumored to have had a weight clause built into their prenuptial agreement. Clients then began asking to incorporate weight-gain penalties into their own documents. To this day, the weight clause is second only to the infidelity clause in popularity with my clients. The weight clause can be built around a monetary penalty for exceeding a certain weight, or it can have lighthearted consequences. Here is an excerpt from an actual weight clause drafted for a high-profile couple:

> *Weight of the Parties. The parties' physical appearance is very important to both of them. They value their active lifestyle and commitment to health. With that in mind, each of the parties agrees to monitor and control his or her weight. In the event that Tina ever gains more than ten (10) pounds, Mark agrees to embark upon a diet program with her. If Mark ever gains more than twenty (20) pounds, Tina agrees to embark upon a diet program with him.*

Tina and Mark were not looking to hold a sledgehammer over each other's heads with the weight clause. Rather, they wanted it to be aspirational and positive in tone. They wanted to get it out there, in writing, what they each felt was a weight danger zone for the other. The consequence, however, wasn't punitive; it was a "team" solution.

Obviously, even a weight clause that has real consequences attached to it must be drafted with flexibility. There must be exceptions made for illness and pregnancy. No matter whether I represent the man or the woman in a love contract, I insist that the weight clause not be in effect from the time a woman is pregnant to one full year after she has given birth. She has enough pressure that first year!

I know firsthand that the weight doesn't magically disappear when the precious bundle is cleaned up and placed in your arms. Unfortunately, Bill (a doctor!) didn't seem to know this. When I was ready to leave the hospital after having my first son, he brought me clothes from home. I wasn't expecting him to have put together any winning fashion combinations. However, I was totally flabbergasted to see a sweater and a prepregnancy pair of size-four jeans in the bag. *What?!* "Should I wear these as a shawl or a hat? Because there is no way I can wear them as pants," I sobbed.

I did manage to lose the baby weight. I credit Vicki Lovine's *Girlfriend's Guide to the First Year of Motherhood* for emphasizing the importance of losing the weight between pregnancies, lest it become much harder to shed later.

THE LOVE CONTRACT FOR SOCIAL MEDIA

For decades, celebrities and other high-powered individuals have required employees, acquaintances, and even wedding guests to sign nondisclosure agreements. This is done in an attempt to prevent anyone given a glimpse under the tent from "dishing the dirt" to the media or anyone else who would listen. Reputational harm to a celebrity has always had the potential to cost them, both in terms of future lost parts as well as penalty-triggering violations of morality clauses contained in network and studio talent agreements.

Today, however, the stakes are higher. Unlike harmful "stories" in years past, we now have to deal with explicit images and their potential for nuclear-level damage. Negative social media content and images have the unique potential to instantaneously derail one's career and, by extension, one's long-term capacity to create wealth. Who can ever forget the image of David Hasselhoff's post–happy hour(s) burger and fries scarfed directly from his kitchen floor? Some of the images I've seen are so distasteful that I feel I have experienced collateral bystander-type damage. Whom can *I* sue to compensate me for the disturbing towel shot of former Congressman Anthony Weiner that I was subjected to? Who can help me delete it from my brain? The answer, of course, is no one. Notwithstanding the help of damage-control consultants and very expensive public relations gurus he reportedly retained, the image is seared into our minds and is immortalized in cyberspace.

Granted, no contractual provision could have prevented Anthony Weiner's predicament, because he was the one who inadvertently sent the bizarre image out there into the virtual universe. His experience did, however, cause me to think about the possibility of vindictive exes intentionally inflicting that type of harm on my clients.

We have all seen people totally lose their capacity for reason in the heat of a breakup. Some people are blinded by rage and are up at night thinking of ways to harm their exes. Who doesn't have embarrassing photos of their ex? What can be done in advance to prevent your ex's index finger from one day moving half an inch and exercising the "nuclear option"? Think she would never go there? Neither did Pat.

PAT AND EVIE'S STORY

Pat and Evie were high school sweethearts. They married within weeks of their college graduation. She worked for a fashion designer, and he landed a job teaching English lit at a private prep school in Manhattan. Two years into the marriage, Pat announced that he had fallen in love with the mother of one of his students. After giving the matter considerable thought, he felt that he owed it to himself to pursue his real chance at happiness. By the time Evie came into my office, her heartbreak had morphed into a warrior-type mindset. Although I knew what the answer was likely to be, I asked Evie if she thought that mediation could work for them. This would save them from an acrimonious court battle, which would, in my opinion, be ridiculous given their modest assets. "No," she replied. "I want to rip his leg from his ass, and I want to do it publicly." All right, then . . . Fortunately for me, I was conflicted out of the case by virtue of having done estate planning work for Pat's family. I heard from them that the judge pushed for a relatively quick settlement.

Evie was disappointed that Pat got out of the marriage and was free to begin a new life so easily. Did anyone care about the public humiliation she had

endured because of him? At some point she remembered
one final hand grenade she could throw. Evie had access
to a very embarrassing video taken of Pat while pledg-
ing a college fraternity. Unfortunately for Pat, she
was able to access the prep school's internal list-
serve. And so it happened that, after a few margaritas
on a Friday evening, Evie emailed the school's entire
board of trustees, faculty, parents, and alumni the
video of a nude Pat French kissing a Belgian sheepdog.

Though some members of the board were sympathetic to
Pat's situation, they explained that they had no choice
but to terminate him. The disseminated image depicted
behavior that very clearly violated the school's morality clause. They did, however, mercifully decide not to
refer the matter to the district attorney for investigation into a potential animal cruelty case.

It is true that we are now living in a different world. For mil-
lennia, people have had their hearts broken. Countless supportive
friends have commiserated with the lovelorn while dutifully insulting the offending party between shots. The difference today, though,
is that these angry and drunken characters all have, in their pants
pocket, embarrassing photos of their exes and a send button that can
inflict career-ending damage.

Thirty-eight states have either enacted or are considering "revenge
porn" legislation. This makes it a potential crime to disseminate nude
or lurid images of another person. These laws would not, however,
prevent the dissemination of content that was merely cripplingly
embarrassing. I believe it is essential to implement a social media
clause within any type of relationship agreement. With monetary
penalties in place, we can ensure that an angry ex can't cause us career
harm for decades to come.

The social media clause can also address potential sources of conflict within an intact relationship. The parties may, for example, have

differing views on the amount and extent of content and images that should be shared with the world. I probably don't want my colleagues and clients seeing unflattering beach pictures of me. My partner, on the other hand, may think that it is harmless fun because he has different criteria for what should be public and what should remain private. This is yet another example of a love contract provision causing a couple to determine what can work for both of them in a given life category.

Another version of a social media clause deals with the amount of time spent on it. Priscilla Chan and Mark Zuckerberg were reported to have agreed within their prenup to a fixed amount of cyber-free time each week.

Here is a sample love contract clause:

ARTICLE 8: SOCIAL MEDIA

8.1 Both parties agree to refrain from any social media activity that will be likely to embarrass the other party. Specifically, the parties agree not to post, text, tweet, email, or otherwise disseminate content intended or likely to hurt the personal or professional reputation of the other. The parties agree to refrain from publicly sharing anecdotes and/or stories about the other if the effect will be public ridicule.

8.2 Both parties agree to refrain from sharing nude or partially nude photos or other images by way of texts, Facebook, Pinterest, Twitter, Instagram, Snapchat, Tumblr, Vine, or any other photo- or video-sharing application. For purposes of this provision, partial nudity shall be defined as unclothed from the waist up or the waist down.

8.3 The parties agree to seek the consent of the other before disseminating any content via social media which may result in the other party's public embarrassment.

8.4 Upon termination of the relationship, each party agrees not to post, upload, or otherwise share via social media any images of or content relating to the other party. This prohibition shall apply to both positive and negative, insulting, or embarrassing content and or images.

Takeaways

Make a threshold decision as to whether the relationship is worthy of repair and improvement. If so, your starting point for a love contract is as follows:

1. What do you want in your relationship? What is your ideal vision of your joint active lifestyle, adventure, wealth-building, cultural and social life, and philanthropic activities? What are your top two or three pet peeves? Be sure to limit these to areas within your partner's control. What do you think your partner will have as his or her pet peeves about you? If you have any known deal breakers, it is a matter of fundamental fairness to let your partner know.
2. What are you willing and unwilling to do to achieve your relationship goals? What steps are you willing to take to try to reduce or eliminate the behaviors that you believe your partner will list as pet peeves? What, if anything, do you feel able and willing to do to insure against the occurrence of your named deal breakers?
3. Collaborate with your partner. What positive goals are in alignment? These will form the starting point for your love contract. Did you correctly guess each other's enumerated pet peeves?
4. If you are utilizing the love contract to deal with serious matters, it may be helpful to enlist a neutral third party to help keep the process free from animus.

13

LOVE CONTRACT
WITH MY FUTURE SELF

When we think of estate planning, our focus tends to be on protecting those who will survive us. We concentrate on minimizing our survivors' taxes, reducing the possibility that they will have conflicts with one another, and even protecting them against their own spendthrift ways. Too often, one's legal planning totally misses the mark in terms of protecting and helping our future selves.

We said earlier that most people's number one fear is public speaking. Right up there near the top of the list is the fear of being elderly. Most people shudder at the thought of being at the mercy of others for all aspects of our daily lives. We know that action is a proven antidote to fear. It follows then that taking action to put

concrete plans in place to shape the course of our future can eliminate some of the fear and stress associated with getting older.

Estate Planning and the Single Girl

Regardless of one's current marital status, I advise all women to view
their estate plan through the eyes of a single person. This is because
the overwhelming majority of us will, at some point, be single. Many
women stay single by choice. For those of us who are married, we
know the divorce rate is between 40 and 50 percent. The rate is even
higher for second (and subsequent) marriages. As for those lucky
couples that "go the distance," 80 percent of women will survive
their husbands (US Census Bureau). This means that women need
to plan for their long-term care and estate planning needs as if they
will, one day, be single.

I encourage my clients to view their estate planning as a series of
answers to this question: What can I do today to improve the quality
of my life fifteen or more years down the road? More specifically, what
written promises can the "me of today" make to the "me of tomorrow"?

Written Promise to My Future Self #1—I Will Shore Up Your Financial Future

I think of every dollar that I waste today as literally being stolen
from the pocket of my future elderly self. Poor saving and spending
habits today will result in a smaller nest egg and quite possibly leave
me financially vulnerable in time to come. This is common sense.
However, good money habits don't come naturally to everyone. At
least, they didn't for me.

When I graduated from law school, I was up to my eyeballs in
student loan and credit card debt. Even though I was lucky enough
to land a job right away, I had difficulty making the minimum

payments on my monthly bills. My spending was out of control. Like many of my peers at the time, I was concerned more with my lifestyle than with building a solid financial future. The decision to stop spending so much was actually made for me—by the three major credit bureaus. I remember being mortified when I was turned down on a BMW lease. After running my credit check, the salesman remarked that I would have difficulty getting financing for a skateboard. This embarrassing episode caused me to think long and hard about the choices that had gotten me to that point and what type of financial future I could expect to have if I didn't turn things around.

I embarked upon a major education that was not part of my financially chaotic childhood. I devoured books by money gurus such as Suze Orman and Robert Kiyosaki. I borrowed these books from the library so as not to further compound my financial problems. I was then ready to make my first promise to my future self that I have never broken: if I cannot comfortably afford the item in question, without borrowing or paying it off over time, *then I don't buy it.* This was the first principle from which my own love contract with my future self was created. I vowed to pay down my debts and build savings. Part of my motivation was the image of returning to the BMW dealership to buy my dream car—in cash. I was on a mission. I became a miser. As a state legislator, it was fairly easy to eat for free. We had a legislator's lounge in the state capital, with endless supplies of cheese, crackers, cut-up vegetables, and instant soup. Meals at home often featured ramen noodles.

It took seven years, but I did it. I paid off every student loan and credit card bill in full. And, I also managed to save the $57,000 for my 5-Series BMW! My euphoria was short-lived, however. I began to analyze my upcoming purchase from the perspective of my future self. Was I doing "her" any favors by trading $57,000 in cash for a car that would go down in value from the moment I left the dealership? I had a tiny grudge against this new voice of reason, because I knew that it would likely keep me from the intoxicating smell of my new dream car. Once I realized that the BMW was not the best thing I could do for my future self, I began to wonder what would be. How could I best invest my new nest egg for the maximum benefit of my future self? Having just read *Rich Dad Poor Dad* and *Real Estate Riches* by Robert Kiyosaki, the decision was easy—real estate!

I bought a two-year-old jeep for $21,000 and used the remaining $36,000 for a down payment on a four-family building in Albany, New York. My monthly net profit after paying the mortgage, taxes, insurance, and water was a little more than $1000. In three years, I recouped the down payment and did it again. Eleven properties later, I know that I made the right decision about the BMW. As tempting as it was at the time, it wasn't an expenditure designed to shore up my financial future.

Written Promise to My Future Self #2—I Will Do Everything Possible to Ensure That Strangers Don't Call the Shots on Any Needed Long-Term Care

We are living longer than ever before. Today, a fifty-year-old woman has an excellent chance of celebrating her ninetieth birthday. Along with this increased lifespan, though, comes a greater chance of developing some medical condition that results in the need for long-term care. Our grandparents were far more likely to die before developing a dementia-related illness or other condition that necessitated personal care assistance. Today's statistics indicate that seven out of ten of us will one day require someone to help us with daily tasks and activities. What are we doing ahead of time to ensure that any future needed care will be provided on our own terms? For most of us, the answer to this question is "nothing."

As we discussed earlier, in the context of second-marriage planning, a dreaded nursing home stay is far more likely when we don't have a personal care plan in place ahead of time. We also need to develop a financial plan, lest the costs of our personal care plan wipe us out. What is the point of working for decades, saving responsibly, and investing intelligently if we don't guard against the very real risk of losing everything in the event long-term care is needed?

MEDICAID

The average cost of a nursing home in the United States exceeds $10,000 per month. In the New York metro area this figure approaches $15,000. It is easy to see how a few years in a nursing home can result in the hemorrhaging of one's life savings. For those who do exhaust all of their own assets, the Medicaid program is the payor of last resort. Medicaid is a shared federal/state program that currently covers most Americans in nursing homes once they have exhausted their assets. Medicaid coverage should not, however, be relied upon as an adequate financial plan. I do not believe that this program will be able to support the crushing long-term care demands of the millions of baby boomers now in or entering their retirement years. The tremendous pressures on federal and state budgets have already resulted in reduced Medicaid availability. In recent years, we have seen the so-called Medicaid look-back period extend from three years to five years. This was done in order to reduce the practice of voluntary divestiture of one's assets to achieve Medicaid financial eligibility. There are now bills in Congress that would increase this look-back period to even longer.

LONG-TERM CARE INSURANCE

For most of us, long-term care insurance is an essential component of our advance planning. It will safeguard assets and also increase the care options available to us later.

When selecting a policy, it is important to compare the proposed daily benefit to the actual daily cost of long-term care facilities in your area. If, for example, the policy covers $150 per day, but nursing homes in your area cost $300 per day, you will still have a big coverage gap later. If you opt for an inflation rider, your daily benefit will grow at the rate of 5 percent per year. However, the actual costs of care increase, on average, 10 percent per year. This is why it is important to select the most comprehensive policy possible. Another important feature to analyze is what percentage of the daily coverage benefit can be used for home care. Even though the $150 coverage amount appears to be mediocre when compared to daily nursing home costs, it can actually provide great home-care coverage.

Clients and friends often ask me to evaluate coverage proposals for them. In addition to looking at what portion of the daily benefit can be used for stay-at-home care, I sometimes question whether it makes sense to cover both husband and wife. Instead of paying two annual premiums for both partners, we explore the advisability of covering only one. In my own case, my husband is twelve years older than I am. As I am educating myself about long-term care insurance options, I am giving serious thought to only buying coverage for myself. Statistically speaking, I will likely be able to help my husband with future needs that he may have—provided that the image of this year's Mother's Day gift (a Starbucks gift card) recedes from my mind. On the other hand, I do not want to burden my two sons or future possible daughters-in-law in time to come.

Most people do not have these policies for a simple reason: they can be quite expensive. Premiums can easily exceed $4,000 per year. Add to this the fact that premiums can increase down the road. If, for example, I pay my premiums for ten years and then they increase to a level I cannot manage, there is no retained value if I decide to drop the coverage.

In recent years, however, new and better long-term care insurance options have become available. There are some hybrid policies that have degrees of "retained value." This means that if you ever decide to let the policy lapse, there will be some cash value returned to you.

Regardless of the specific plan you select, having long-term care coverage will give you peace of mind now and will prevent your loved ones and future self from stressing over which assets need to be sold off to pay for needed care later. This coverage is a great way of taking care of your future self and, therefore, qualifies as an integral feature of your love contract with your future self.

Perhaps even more challenging than identifying a payment source is appointing the person or persons who will be in charge of communicating our future care preferences to a physician or other health-care provider.

HEALTH-CARE PROXY

The laws of every state allow you to appoint another individual to make health-care decisions on your behalf in the event that you are ever unable to communicate your own wishes. This document does not have to be done by a lawyer. Your state's department of health probably has the template available on their website. The proxy has to be signed in the presence of two witnesses. Most states limit the agent to one person acting at a time. You can name a primary agent and then a back-up agent who has authority to take over decision-making if the primary agent is, for any reason, unable to act. In order for your agent to have unlimited authority, you need to specify that they have your permission to decide later "whether or not to withhold artificial nutrition and/or life-sustaining treatment." The word "whether" indicates that you are not necessarily deciding in advance that you want certain care withheld. You are simply authorizing your named agent to determine whether or not to possibly withhold care later. It is also a good idea to include your named agent's cell phone number on the document.

You should also specify your wishes regarding hydration and pain medication on the health-care proxy. Even those of us who may not wish to be kept alive through extraordinary means may wish to be kept hydrated and as free from pain as possible. This statement regarding pain medication alleviates some liability concerns on the part of medical providers that, too often, can result in inadequate end-of-life pain management.

Beyond these specifications, it is important to avoid our inner control freak's impulse to load the health-care proxy up with a lot of additional information. At its core, a "proxy" is a pure delegation of authority. If I load this document up with a lot of rules and restrictions, I am actually undercutting the unlimited authority of my named agent.

The living will, by contrast, can and should contain your specific wishes and preferences. An example follows:

LIVING WILL DECLARATION

Declaration made this _____ day of _____ , _____
                     (date)   (month)   (year)

I, JANE SMITH, residing at _____ City,
_____ State, _____ Zip, being of sound mind, will-
fully and voluntarily make known my desires that my dying
shall not be artificially prolonged under the circumstances set forth below, and do declare:

If at any time I should have an incurable injury, disease, or illness certified to be a terminal condition
by two (2) physicians who have personally examined
me, one of whom shall be my attending physician, and
the physicians have determined that my death will
occur whether or not life-sustaining procedures are
utilized and where the application of life-sustaining
procedures would serve only to artificially prolong
the dying process, I direct that such procedures be
withheld or withdrawn, and that I be permitted to die
naturally with only the administration of medication
or the performance of any medical procedure deemed
necessary to provide me with comfort, care, or to
alleviate pain.

In the absence of my ability to give directions
regarding the use of such life-sustaining procedures,
it is my intention that this declaration shall be
honored by my family and physician(s) as the final
expression of my legal right to refuse medical or surgical treatment and accept the consequences from such
refusal.

I understand the full import of this declaration,
and I am emotionally and mentally competent to make
this declaration.

JANE SMITH

I believe the declarant to be of sound mind. I did not
sign the declarant's signature above for, or at the
direction of, the declarant. I am at least 18 years of
age and am not related to the declarant by blood or
marriage, entitled to any portion of the estate of the
declarant according to the laws of intestate succes-
sion of the State of _____ or under any will of the
declarant or codicil thereto, or directly financially
responsible for declarant's medical care. I am not
the declarant's attending physician, an employee of
the attending physician, or an employee of the health
facility in which the declarant is a patient.

Witness #1 _____ Residing
at _____
Witness #2 _____ Residing
at _____

You are free to customize the language in the Living Will. I
encourage you to share your ideas for possible use by others. One
anonymous submission follows:

> Last night, my kids and I were sitting in the living room and I said
> to them, "I never want to live in a vegetative state, dependent on
> some machine and fluids from a bottle. If that ever happens, just
> pull the plug." They got up, unplugged the computer, and threw
> out my chardonnay! The little bastards.

Lame joking aside, the living will should be as specific and creative as your imagination allows. I encourage my clients to list their
favorite foods. In the event that a dementia-related illness causes

me to forget the word pizza, I am inclined to think I will still like to eat it.

Written Promise to My Future Self #3—I Will Do Everything Possible to Keep You Out of a Nursing Home

My living will contains the following clause: "In the event that I ever require long-term care, I wish for my care to be provided in my home unless it is medically impracticable or otherwise inadvisable."

When given the choice, most of us have a strong preference to be cared for in our own homes. Compared to a nursing facility, one's home environment offers some clear advantages. For instance, you have greater control over the menu. You aren't subjected to a roommate blaring game shows or soap operas over a shared television. You can select—and fire—your caregiver.

Studies have shown that care in one's home can lead to better outcomes. This is especially true for people suffering from cognitive impairments such as dementia-related illnesses.

Admittedly, there are times when care in a facility is unavoidable. When one requires rehabilitation following a hospitalization or ventilator care, a facility is probably better equipped to provide the care. However, after having worked with thousands of families navigating long-term care, I believe that many nursing home residents could be better cared for at home.

It is the failure to arm oneself with information in advance of a crisis that often leads to the "nursing home by default" selection in an emergency. Adult children often decide to have Mom remain in the rehab/nursing home for "an extra month" while they arrange for home care and make any needed modifications to the home. Unfortunately, this extra month often results in a mental and physical decline, which, in turn, can require extended stay in the nursing home.

There are some relatively easy steps one can take in order to maximize the chances of receiving care at home. The first step is to inform your loved ones and health-care proxy agent. This can be done verbally but is more likely to be honored if in writing.

I also recommend that you making an annually updated list of professionals who make home visits. These include physicians, dentists, physical therapists, accountants, attorneys, and geriatric care managers.

Next, consider whether any physical modifications are necessary for the home. You may also investigate the new technologies that reduce feelings of isolation. We've come a long way from simple pendant buttons that alert the world to a fall. Currently available interactive technologies allow families to have visual and voice access to loved ones from anywhere in the world.

Your collection of home-care information, together with your specific wishes, forms the basis of your personal home-care plan. Once assembled, your home-care plan should be kept in a folder in your home, and a copy should be kept in your elder law attorney's file. Now, in the event of hospitalization, your loved ones will have some concrete action steps to take. This will maximize your ability to receive your care in your home.

REVERSE MORTGAGES

There is a widespread perception that reverse mortgages are some type of scam. I happen to be a fan of them, provided that one has all of the facts. For seniors who are "real estate rich" and cash poor, the reverse mortgage is a way to "live on" some of the home's equity while remaining where they want to be. It is often the better financial choice to selling and "downsizing."

For seniors who don't qualify for traditional mortgages or a home-equity loan because they don't have a high statistical likelihood of working another thirty years, the reverse mortgage allows them to borrow against their house in whatever amount they choose, up to a fixed percentage of the home's fair market value. There are no monthly payments to be made. Instead, the entire amount borrowed is due upon the earlier of the sale of the home or the homeowner's death, whichever occurs first.

What are the downsides? There are significant closing costs. These have been lowered by the Reverse Mortgage Stabilization Act of 2013, but they are still higher than a traditional mortgage. The interest rate is also higher. One way to keep this down is to structure the payment as a line of credit. This way, the borrower is only accruing interest on what he or she actually uses as opposed to the entire loan amount.

When I suggest the reverse mortgage as a possible option to my clients who are considering downsizing, I hear a common objection: but I don't want the kids to get less when I die. My response is that the kids would also get less if you downsize and live on the difference between the two properties. That's the reason you are thinking about downsizing in the first place.

Let's look at Marge's options. She lives in a house worth $600,000. She is considering selling it to move into a condo that will cost $300,000. Is this a wise move? Financially speaking, probably not. She will pay at least 3 percent in commission ($18,000) to a real estate broker on the sale. There may also be capital gains tax consequences. If Marge purchased the home for $50,000 in 1977, she has a built-in capital gain of $550,000. This is reduced by $250,000 because she lived there as her primary residence for two out of the past five years. The long-term capital gain on the resulting $300,000 will still be more than $45,000 depending upon her state of residence. If, instead, she is able to hold onto the home until death, her children will receive it with a so-called "step up in basis" (Internal Revenue Code sec. 1015), meaning that they will inherit it with no capital gains tax consequences. There are also legal fees for both the sale and purchase (about $1,000 for each). Because the condo is likely to be newer, chances are that the annual real estate taxes are higher. Add to this monthly maintenance fees associated with a condo or co-op, and the numbers look even worse. Finally, selling the house will deprive Marge's heirs of the continued appreciation on the property. Every year, in that neighborhood, home values rise by about 3 percent. Wouldn't the condo or a smaller house also appreciate? Yes, but the 3 percent appreciation gain each year would only apply to the lower $300,000 value. For me, the lynchpin in the entire analysis is that one continues to benefit from the appreciation on the entire fair market value of the house—even that portion of it that is subject to the reverse mortgage. By contrast, the reverse mortgage interest only applies to the smaller amount borrowed.

It is a different analysis entirely if the house has simply become too much for Marge to manage. Moving would also make sense if her friends have moved away and she is isolated because she no longer drives. Marge absolutely should consider moving if it will likely enhance her quality of life. I just don't want anyone to think that selling and downsizing is necessarily a good financial move.

Written Promise to My Future Self #4—I Will Do Everything Possible to Protect You from Scam Artists and Evildoers

As an estate attorney, I know that I have seen the very best and the very worst of human nature. I have seen favored children willingly share their inheritances with brothers and sisters. I have seen clients live frugally so that their ultimate charitable beneficiaries receive more later. I have facilitated organ donation requests and have seen countless clients open their homes to relatives and strangers without blinking an eye. On the flip side, I have seen the worst of the worst. I am always amazed to see new lows in human depravity as it relates to relieving others of their money and assets.

ANNA DOOLEY'S STORY

Ten years ago, a client was referred to me by a local funeral director who handled her preplanning. Anna Dooley required a home visit because she didn't drive and was too frail to navigate public transportation. Miss Dooley was seventy-eight years old, never married, and was still living in her childhood home that she and her recently deceased sister, Theresa, had

shared. This was one of the most amazing houses I had
ever seen. The furniture was her grandparents', and
unlike similar pieces that I've seen at antique stores
and estate sales, Miss Dooley's furniture was entirely
free from the many little nicks, dings, scrapes, and
spills caused by children. I felt like I was in a
museum, with the exception of the least attractive dog
I had ever laid eyes upon. Cookie was a small uniden-
tifiable breed with large bald spots and no teeth on
account of her penchant for Mallomars and licorice.
Getting down to the business at hand, Miss Dooley
advised me that she needed to change her will now that
her sole beneficiary, Theresa, was gone. I asked her
if there were friends and/or charities that she wished
to include in her estate. Miss Dooley responded that
she wished to leave everything to her church. This
seemed perfectly plausible to me, given the fact that
she was a religious woman and went to church daily.
As an aside, does it matter whether her beneficiary
selection was plausible to me or not? Isn't my job to
simply take down her wishes and incorporate them into
a will? Sort of. Whenever I am dealing with people who
have just suffered a major blow, I try to be sensitive
to whether they are looking at things rationally and
especially whether there may be nefarious characters
around who are trying to call the shots. Elderly people who live alone tend to be catnip to scammers.

Satisfied that everything seemed normal, I created
the new will and returned to her home a few weeks later
with two members of my office staff to act as witnesses. They were both simultaneously charmed by Miss
Dooley and horrified by the sight of the dog.

Once the will was completed, I didn't hear from
Miss Dooley again for several years. Then, I received
a call from a Mr. Peter Traficant, who identified

himself as a friend of hers. He went on to *tell* me
that I was to change Miss Dooley's will to leave him
the house. I resisted my initial impulse to hang up
on him for fear that he would have some other attorney make the change. Instead, I summoned all of my
political PR skills and explained that, as a matter
of law, I needed to meet with my client personally
in order to commence changes to an existing will.
I suggested that Miss Dooley call me directly to
make an appointment. Well, I can only imagine that
he shoved her into his car at that moment, because
they appeared at my office within the hour. I greeted
them in the reception area and had to stop Peter
from tagging along when I escorted Miss Dooley into
the conference room. I told him that it was a legal
"technicality" that required me to meet alone with my
client. Once safely behind closed doors, I asked my
lovely client, "Who on earth is this guy?"

"I am not quite sure" she replied. "He has been
coming around to help me with odd jobs and goes to the
store for me."

"What about the business with the house?" I asked.

She explained that she would prefer to keep her
will the way that it was with everything going to the
church but felt that she was in a quandary. Appar-
ently, Peter had told her that if she left him the
house, he would promise to let Cookie continue living
there without disruption.

Knowing how much she loved that crazy little dog, I
understood the appeal of this jerk's proposal to her.
Then and there, I promised to ensure that Cookie would
find a nice home in the event that the dog survived
her. I further promised that the dog would come home
with me if there were no other options. As much as I
cringed at the thought of this alien-looking creature

coming home with me, I felt that there was no choice. She believed me but didn't know what she should say to Peter after our meeting. I suggested that she tell Peter whatever she wanted (including a white lie that she made the change he wanted) in order to get him to stop badgering her. Most original wills are normally kept in my vault, so it would be understandable that she wouldn't have the document to show him.

My ingenuity, it turned out, was no match for this scoundrel. About a year after their office visit, I received a weird call from a secretary in another law firm. She refused to share her name for fear of losing her job. She wanted to tell me that my "former" client, Miss Dooley, was in their office recently to change her estate planning documents. The secretary went out on a limb by calling me, because she wanted someone to know that something was not quite right. She told me that Miss Dooley appeared to be confused and agitated. I thanked her and promised to see what could be done.

I promptly called our local Adult Protective Services agency and they commenced an investigation. It turned out that the evil Peter had not only managed to have Miss Dooley's will changed, but he had also had himself named as her power of attorney. With this document, he then transferred ownership of the beautiful family home into his own name! The matter was referred to the district attorney's office and ended with Peter returning the home and other assets that Miss Dooley had no memory of "gifting" to him. He also agreed to a lifetime ban on contacting her in exchange for dropping criminal charges. The story did not have an entirely happy ending, however. By this point, Miss Dooley was deemed by a court to lack the mental capacity necessary to handle her own affairs. Because of this, a judge appointed a "guardian" who was now in charge of all of Miss Dooley's affairs. Granted, no amount of advance planning could have prevented her from developing a cognitive impairment, but she could have and should have had a springing power of attorney in place ahead of time. This would have prevented a judge from selecting a stranger to fill this role.

Anna's story emphasized for me how vulnerable we are when living by ourselves in later years. Because of this, I encourage everyone to contemplate building a team of "eyes and ears" that can insulate us from evildoers in years to come as well as handle our affairs and finances in the event that we are ever unable to do so.

Within the context of the love contract with our future selves, we can begin the process of recruiting and assembling a team of people who can "keep an eye out" for possible problems in years to come. Without a natural ready-made team, one's physician, attorney, accountant, or geriatric care manager can fill this role. Hospital discharge planning departments can often be a good source to recommend caring and competent professionals and organizations in your area. I recommend "interviewing" these people in advance to determine whether there is a good rapport.

It is far better to assemble your team ahead of time, lest some strange judge's golf buddy be appointed to handle your affairs. If you have no ideal candidates in your personal life, then I recommend a second "recruiting" process. A trusted friend, clergy member, or financial professional may be a good start. To promote accountability, you may wish to name two people acting together. You can also reduce the scope of your agent's power within your documents to guard against the possibility of wrongdoing.

Ideally, you will sit down with each of your chosen care team members once a year to discuss future care and financial management plans. It is important to draft flexible documents so that you can replace your named agents whenever you wish. Once you take the smallest first step on this planning process, I promise that you will feel more empowered as you look toward the future.

Having gained mastery over my finances and having set up legal structures to ensure that any needed care is delivered on my terms, I believe I am definitely doing the right thing by my future self.

Takeaways

1. Consider steps you can take today to promote the financial security and well-being of the "you" fifteen years down the road.
2. If you can't afford to buy something today without financing it—then don't buy it today. Don't saddle your future self with the tab for today's purchases.
3. Determine how you would wish to receive any future possible long-term care.
4. Determine who should make health-care and financial decisions for you in the event that you can't. Memorialize these decisions within a health-care proxy and power of attorney.
5. Make a plan to pay for any future possible long-term care. This should include an investigation of long-term care insurance options.
6. Develop a network of trusted advisors who can act as your eyes and ears down the road. This network of family, friends, or professionals can help ensure that the future you isn't victimized by scam artists.

14

THE LOVE CONTRACT WITH
FUTURE GENERATIONS

Have you ever thought about your parting words to friends, family, and the world? In theory, most would agree that our last words should convey the full measure of our love for those we are leaving. Ideally, our words would also impart courage, wisdom, humor, and solace. We would distill our life experiences into guiding principles and commit this to writing for those who follow.

Unfortunately, for the vast majority of us, our final words are limited to those contained in the last will and testament. The content of this document has changed surprisingly little over the course of many centuries. Your will is probably identical to that of your next-door neighbor. That's because most lawyers preparing wills simply cut and paste names into a standard template. Is this really the best we can do for our grieving loved ones and future descendants?

The word "testament" is derived from the Greek and literally means "statement of beliefs." "Will" means deliberate choice. So "last will and testament" really means one's last deliberately chosen beliefs. Were these the treasures originally intended to be passed down through the will? Researching this query led me on a literary journey back to the Middle Ages.

Hebrew ethical wills were used for centuries to transmit moral guidance to future generations. They had a continuous presence throughout early Jewish literature up to the early part of the twentieth century. At that time, Dr. Israel Abrahams, reader of Rabbinics at the University of Cambridge, set about compiling and translating these documents. A survey of his work reveals a varied compilation of moral guides written by fathers for their sons.

Some of the ethical wills were written and added to over the course of many years. Others were transcripts of the dying man's verbal exhortations to his family. The advice imparted ranged from the mundane ("My Son! Drink no water that has been left uncovered overnight.") to the beneficent ("My Son! Give unto thy Creator His share of all thy food . . . This, God's portion belongs to the poor.").

Learning about Hebrew ethical wills inspired me to take this to the next level by setting up a two-way exchange between my clients and future generations. These love contracts with the future are now a standard part of my law practice. What exchange of value can there be across generations? How can you enter a contract with those you will never meet? Ask yourself what you wouldn't give to receive some advice or words of encouragement from an ancestor who lived, laughed, struggled, cried, and died on this very earth stage generations ago. There is nothing that I wouldn't give to receive this gift. That is how I know that sending a message forward can definitely transmit something of value.

One's final words are accorded a special value as legal evidence, because we all agree that when faced with death, we express the truth. Some special people among us, when faced with imminent death, manage to share deeply principled and inspirational messages with the world. Who can help but be inspired by Daniel Pearl's last message when he was about to be beheaded by terrorists: "My father's Jewish, my mother's Jewish, I'm Jewish." I was deeply moved by these words. I have also derived courage and perspective from them on more than one occasion in my own life. When expressed truths transmit something of value, I believe that the recipient is inspired to "pay it forward." Do I think Daniel Pearl meant to speak to me? Certainly not. He did, however, give me something of value that has elevated my sensibilities. In turn, I am inspired to take action that will help give others a boost. If he only had the time to suggest specific actions I might take to help others, I would do so in a heartbeat.

A valid contract requires a two-way exchange. What can I ask of people I will never meet? The possibilities here are truly limitless. We can start by coming up with five actions we wish for our descendants to take in order to protect the environment, improve their communities, etc. This can be an empowering and ennobling tool.

Why have we gotten away from sharing our values and beliefs in our last communication to loved ones? For many, it seems to be too daunting a task. There is enormous pressure for the words and ideas to be perfect. The desire for a perfect love contract with the future usually results in no love contract. The human condition causes us to believe that there is an infinite amount of time for every task on life's to-do list. Giving final words of guidance to our surviving loved ones and future generations is one more thing that we will get around to "someday."

If you are willing to abandon the pursuit of perfection and are willing to start somewhere, here are some action steps to follow.

Unlike a regular will, there is no special format that must be followed for your love contract with the future. I do recommend that the love contract provisions be separate from your regular will. Having a separate document reduces confusion and also allows you to direct when it will be shared with your loved ones. You may request that your attorney or trusted friend hold the document and share it after a prescribed period of time after death. This will enable the family to deal with all of the property and legal issues before they receive your true legacy.

A good starting point is to come up with some lessons you have learned that you wish you had come upon sooner. Some examples of love contracts with the future follow. The first is in the form of a letter created by a forty-two-year-old cancer patient.

Love Contract with the Future #1

Dear Loved Ones,

As I thought about all of you, I could feel your love for me and I want you to know that sustained me during some pretty bleak hours. Thoughts of your compassion and humanity have given me a boost. Unfortunately, there wasn't time to for me to thank all of you and say goodbye in person, so I hope you will forgive the group missive as I try to share with you some of the truths that have occurred to me since my diagnosis last year.

I have profoundly experienced that love is all that matters. Like many people, I often got caught up in my pettiness and separation, thinking I was always right. I judged others and I have judged myself even more harshly. But I have learned that we carry within ourselves the abundant wisdom and love to heal our weary hearts and judgmental minds.

During the time of my illness, I have come to realize that we are all doing the best we can. Judging others closes the heart and lowers our personal energy level. My new definition of a successful life is how we express love for ourselves and others. I realize that I was so judgmental of others for so long because I was fundamentally disappointed with myself. I often placed my own career and personal ambitions above the feelings of others. Looking back now, I realize that I was partially crippled by fear my entire life. My biggest fear was probably what others thought of me. Sounds crazy, I know. I viewed my every action and decision through the prism of how I thought others would judge me. In the category of better late than never, I can honestly say that I am finally free of this fear. Only two of you here today know that when I was eighteen, I gave my newborn up for adoption. No, I wasn't really studying art in Florence that year! Although I rationalized at the time that it was the best decision both for my baby and myself, I often felt self-hatred and profound sadness over this. I believe now that my decision to give up my beautiful baby was also motivated, in large part, by what I thought others would think of me as a struggling unemployed single mother. Could I have really given up my baby because I didn't want all of you to think I was a loser? That is sad. Dying does not give me any new or special clarity with which to resolve these feelings. I do realize, though, that we all have these "unresolvable" elements in our minds and hearts. My hope for all of you here today is that you let go of the fears that may be holding you back and give yourselves a big pass on perfectly mastering every aspect of your inner lives. No, that doesn't mean that you have to stop seeing your therapists! Rather, I urge you to focus on the areas of your lives and our world that you do have the power to elevate by your words, actions, and thoughts.

If I had more time on this earth I would take the time to apologize to those of you I have hurt and offended. I would finally take action on my perennial New Year's resolution to volunteer and support the ASPCA. If any of these words I have shared today resonate with you, or inspire you to live your life more authentically, may I be so presumptuous as to ask you to do something in return? My request is that you help the ASPCA or your local animal shelter in whatever way you can. My grand vision is that a pet charity becomes financially strong enough to connect with elderly "pet parents" of limited means and help them care for their pets.

I know with every fiber of my being that many of you will rise to the occasion. This enables me to count your actions in this regard as my own and fills me with a sense of great accomplishment. My heart feels as if it has exploded with gratitude to you for this. I no longer carry anger, fear, or critical thoughts.

As I stand (figuratively—trust me) at the end of "the parade," I choose to focus my thoughts on the puppies and kittens that you will allow "me" to rescue.

I urge you all to look back over your own lives and distill a few guiding principles, words of advice, and perhaps a request or two for those who will survive you—the bombshell confession is optional. Writing this has been a cathartic and uplifting experience. I hope that you do this while you still have the physical strength to hold a pen.

Life is not about how long we live, but about how we live, and I have had a good life. I accept my dying as part of the beautiful and mysterious process of life. My sadness is in leaving you. I'll miss the deep comfort and love of waking up in Michael's arms, giving up our dreams of babies and future years together. I'll miss the sunny days of fishing with my dad, of sharing with my mom her love of life and selfless nature. I'll miss giggling with my sister Barbara over life's impasses.

As I lay dying, I think of all of you, each special in your own way, that I have loved and shared this life with. I reluctantly give up walking on this beautiful planet, where every step is a gift. The glistening sun on the mountains, the sound of a brook as it makes its way over rocks, the purity and magic of the season's first snowfall, Paris in springtime, and a dry martini☺—these are the things I have loved.

Please do not think I have lost a battle with my disease, for I have won the challenge of life. I have shared unconditional love. I have opened to the mystery of Spirit and feel that divinity is all around us every day and provides us with a path on which our spirit may take flight.

When you think of me, know that my spirit has taken flight and that I love you.

—Jill

Love Contract with the Future #2

Putting these words on paper feels a little bit like letting go of a helium balloon or sending a paper boat sailing down a stream. I know that I will not be there for the end result. In this case, I will not be there when these words are read by all of you. It is strange and yes, depressing, to imagine a world without ME in it! But, as I have learned over the course of the past several months, from more specialists than I care to recall, my "leg" of life's big relay race is ending. I haven't given up all hope just yet. I have been approved to take part in a study using an experimental medication. I have also dusted off my juicing machine and am reading books about the healing powers of positive thinking. During a recent check-up though, it was "suggested" that I may want to put my affairs in order so that I "could focus on my recovery." Stupidity never being one of my many flaws, I am now in the process of updating my estate planning documents.

In addition to my regular will to "whack up my stuff," my attorney suggested creating this "love contract with the future." The way I understand it is that I try to give you, dear future readers, some valuable near-death-inspired pearls of wisdom that you may incorporate into your own lives. I then get to ask you to do something for me only if you feel that I have given you anything helpful or useful. This "contract" requires a two-way exchange. This seemed to me to be a bit contrived at first, but I welcomed the break from researching my disease and drinking my green juice, so I began to think.

I do feel as though I have gained some remarkable insights, as I have had a great deal of time to reflect back over the course of the past fifty-three years. I think about things I am proud of as well as many things I would have done differently. I see and feel with an almost 3D capacity all of the times I was unkind to someone. As I look back, it seems that I was always in a hurry. I was (very) often impatient with my family, coworkers, and strangers. I was completely intolerant of others' weaknesses, because I had suffered so many setbacks in my own life and never let them stand in the way of my success. I never sat around feeling sorry for myself. I never sat on the couch crying into a bowl of chips after a breakup or career problem. Nope, not me. I never felt sorry for myself, so why should I feel sorry for someone else?

Then I began questioning the wisdom of never feeling sorry for myself. What does it mean to feel sorry for oneself? For the first time in my life, I looked up the word. Turns out that sorry means "feeling or expressing sympathy or compassion." Huh. If we substitute the word compassion for sorrow, things begin to shift. By steadfastly avoiding feeling sorry for myself, I was simultaneously avoiding feeling sympathy or compassion for myself. By extension, if I feel no compassion for myself, how in the world can I be expected to feel it for other people? How could I have possibly been kind and loving to the world if I refused any sympathy for myself? We all know that we are supposed to treat others the way we want to be treated. The converse is just as true. I believe that we can't be expected to treat others well if we don't start treating ourselves well.

Viewed from that perspective, feeling sorry for oneself seems less self-indulgent and more like a first step to being a kinder and more nurturing person. How could that be a bad thing? Dare I "go there" now, though? I mean now, I really do have a lot to feel sorry for myself about. Then I figured that things couldn't get much worse, so I thought about why I was sorry that I would probably not be here much longer:

I thought about how &!#@ing UNFAIR this is. I finally allowed myself to think about missing out on my future plans and goals. Except for my goal to lose a few pounds (gallows humor). I thought about the vacations I won't get to take; missing my kids' weddings. I thought about saying goodbye to Jeffrey, my high school sweetheart and the love of my life. Yes, I want him to find the future happiness that he deserves, and yes, I know that will probably involve another woman (though he denies it now). Just this once, though, I allowed myself to feel the profound grief that the image of my kids at his future wedding conjures up. I allowed myself to fully feel ANGER and SORROW. Did I mention how &!#@ing UNFAIR this is?

I think I cried for an entire day and then, yes, I did feel better. I felt lighter. Less martyrlike and without the weight of the world on my shoulders. Freed up from my stoicism, I do feel more love and compassion for myself and everyone around me.

I don't happen to believe in reincarnation. So I don't feel like I will be able to carry these major life insights into my next life with me. Perhaps in a few more weeks as desperation and pain meds increase, I may be of a different opinion. For now, though, I can only share my advice with you, who have survived me:

My hope for all of you is that you will be kinder to yourselves. I believe that this includes feeling sorry for yourself from time to time. This doesn't mean that you should wallow in pity for days on end or blow off work or school or other commitments. This means that you should focus more on your feelings and engage in activities that promote your happiness. From my perspective, kindness to yourself enables you to be kinder to those around you. This is far more important than bank account balances or other arbitrary measures of success. If only I didn't waste so much time chasing my tail to achieve the latter, I would, ironically, feel more like a success right now.

If this advice resonates with you and you feel inspired to use any of it as you continue on own life's journey, I now ask that you consider doing something in exchange:

One of my life plans was to become more involved with St. Jude Children's Hospital. I was a monthly sponsor for the past twenty years and made a provision for them in my will. I am now asking that you consider supporting their very worthy efforts in any manner that you are able. Please consider visiting their website: www.stjude.org. I know in my heart that many of you will rise to the occasion. As I think of the children and babies that will be helped because of our "contract," I feel like I was an instrument of "good." I thank you in advance for allowing me to leave the stage, a success!

With Peace and Love,
Abigail

A variation on the love contract with the future is to use a specific action, as opposed to words of wisdom, as the thing of value that we transmit into the future. Here, our contract informs the future reader of a specific action we've taken. This could be planting a tree or organizing a beach cleanup. We let the future reader know we did this thing in order to promote his health by way of a greener environment. We then get to ask him to consider doing something that we would like to see continued in the future.

I often find myself feeling "in debt" to those who have improved the world in concrete ways. William Van Alen, for example, who designed the iconic Chrysler Building, has brought joy to millions. Surely, if he had left a written request for future generations, I would do my best to fulfill it as repayment for the visual benefit he gave to "me." Without a specific written request, we can try to imagine what actions those who came before us would want us to take. Whenever I am in Central Park, I am in awe of the foresight of Theodore Roosevelt in ensuring that this spectacular space would be preserved for future generations. As a member of one of the many generations who succeeded Mr. Roosevelt, I know, in a general sense, that he would want me to pick up any cup, can, or food wrapper strewn about the park. I also imagine that he would want me to support the efforts of the Central Park Conservancy, whose mission it is to preserve and enhance the park. I joined this group in large part to "earn" or deserve the benefit that the park has given me. Rather than guess at what he'd want me to do, though, I feel he had every right in the world to ask future generations to undertake specific actions as a way of projecting his efforts far and wide into the modern era.

It is in this spirit that I encourage you to take an action designed to make the world a healthier and/or more beautiful place in as concrete a manner as possible. You then get to ask people you will never meet to do world-enhancing things for people they may never meet.

Takeaways

1. A standard will alone is a pitiful last form of communication to love ones.
2. Consider creating an ethical will. This is a document separate from your regular will that sets forth a few life lessons and guiding principles that have shaped your world view.
3. Your ethical will can make the leap to a love contract by setting up a type of two-way exchange between yourself and future generations.
4. The love contract can be created by projecting life lessons to a future reader who, in return, is asked to take a specific action to help the world that he or she inhabits.
5. Alternatively, we can let a future reader know about a concrete action we've taken to beautify or clean up the world. In return for what we did, we ask them to take a similar action.

EPILOGUE

It is my hope that the information presented in these pages will encourage you to implement a few legal structures to protect yourself from life's inevitable curveballs. I hope that you will think creatively and develop estate planning structures that do so much more than simply whack up your stuff upon breakup or at death. I hope that you are now more sensitized to the wealth-eroding potential of low mojo and troubled relationships. I hope that you take steps to prevent explosive collisions between your loved ones and your money. I hope that you will commit to becoming more secure and prosperous, and that you have many healthy years to share your wealth with your loved ones, on your own terms. Last, I hope that you will consider joining me in making a contract with future generations. If you wish to share this document with me (and the world!), please contact me at www.mylawyerann.com.

INDEX

Books from Allworth Press

Estate Planning for the Healthy, Wealthy Family
by Carla Garrity, Mitchell Baris, and Stanley Neeleman (6 x 9, 256 pages, ebook, $22.99)

Feng Shui and Money
by Eric Shaffert (6 x 9, 256 pages, paperback, $16.95)

How to Plan and Settle Estates
by Edmund Fleming (6 x 9, 288 pages, paperback, $16.95)

Legal Forms for Everyone, Sixth Edition
by Carl W. Battle (8 ½ x 11, 280 pages, paperback, $24.99)

Legal Guide to Social Media
by Kimberly A. Houser (6 x 9, 208 pages, paperback, $19.95)

Living Trusts for Everyone, Second Edition
by Ronald Farrington Sharp (5 ½ x 8 ¼, 192 pages, paperback, $14.99)

The Money Mentor
by Tad Crawford (6 x 9, 272 pages, paperback, $24.95)

Protecting Your Assets from Probate and Long-Term Care
by Evan H. Farr (5 ½ x 8 ¼, 208 pages, paperback, $14.99)

Scammed
by Gini Graham Scott, PhD (6 x 9, 256 pages, paperback, $14.99)

The Secret Life of Money
by Tad Crawford (5 ½ x 8 ½, 304 pages, paperback, $19.95)

The Smart Consumer's Guide to Good Credit
by John Ulzheimer (5 ¼ x 8 ¼, 216 pages, paperback, $14.95)

Your Living Trust & Estate Plan, Fifth Edition
by Harvey J. Platt (6 x 9, 352 pages, paperback, $16.95)

To see our complete catalog or to order online, please visit *www.allworth.com*.